REDNECK
RESILIENCE

JAMES HAROLD WEBB

REDNECK
RESILIENCE

A COUNTRY BOY'S JOURNEY
TO PROSPERITY

Advantage.

Published by Advantage, Charleston, South Carolina.
Member of Advantage Media Group.

ADVANTAGE is a registered trademark, and the Advantage colophon is a trademark of Advantage Media Group, Inc.

Printed in the United States of America.

10 9 8 7 6 5 4 3 2 1

ISBN: 978-1-64225-239-2
LCCN: 2021901705

Cover design by David Taylor.
Layout design by Mary Hamilton.

This publication is designed to provide accurate and authoritative information in regard to the subject matter covered. It is sold with the understanding that the publisher is not engaged in rendering legal, accounting, or other professional services. If legal advice or other expert assistance is required, the services of a competent professional person should be sought.

 Advantage Media Group is proud to be a part of the Tree Neutral® program. Tree Neutral offsets the number of trees consumed in the production and printing of this book by taking proactive steps such as planting trees in direct proportion to the number of trees used to print books. To learn more about Tree Neutral, please visit **www.treeneutral.com**.

Advantage Media Group is a publisher of business, self-improvement, and professional development books and online learning. We help entrepreneurs, business leaders, and professionals share their Stories, Passion, and Knowledge to help others Learn & Grow. Do you have a manuscript or book idea that you would like us to consider for publishing? Please visit **advantagefamily.com** or call **1.866.775.1696**.

To my children: Elizabeth, Maxwell, Joseph, Kristen, and Carly. Brought together by circumstances beyond your control, the love and commitment to family that all of you have shown is the reason we continue on this gracious, yet necessary, path. I believe in each of you and know that this journey together will lead to a brighter future for the next generations and an ability to give back to others in a way I never imagined. I love you guys. Now go get 'em!

CONTENTS

ACKNOWLEDGMENTS

I want to acknowledge, and thank, those people who have helped shape me into the person I am today.

To Craig Heimbuch: What a fun ride we had writing this book together. Your assistance, guidance, and ability to help me translate my story was awesome. I hope the next "chapter" in your life leads you down a path of fun, growth, and prosperity. Thank you.

To my parents, Jimmy Webb and Jane Johnson: I cannot fathom what it must have been like having a child at eighteen years of age, but I am so grateful that you accepted this responsibility with commitment, grace, and love. Dad, you are the most honest, hardworking human being I know, and I am honored to be your son. The life lessons I have learned from your actions are forever engrained in my soul. Mom, your relentless and tireless spirit as a parent will never be forgotten. Managing our household while going back to college was truly awe inspiring for my brothers and me. Both of you are the cornerstones that have made me into the person I am today and the single biggest reason for my success.

To Eve Webb: Thank you for loving and caring for my dad and for being an integral part of our family. It continues to be a fun ride with no end in sight! Love ya.

To my brothers, Ronney Joe and Chris: I will always be there for you as you have been there for me. So proud of each of you and your ongoing successes and achievements. Go get 'em, boys, like I know you can.

To Margaret Love Crosby: As my fourth- and sixth-grade teacher, you have forever left an imprint on me and on so many others you have taught. Through you, I learned the value of education. Through you, I learned that teachers can, and do, care. Through you, I learned that we are all equal as human beings and must strive to build a better place for our descendants regardless of race, ethnicity, religion, or gender. Thank you for being the coolest teacher I ever had!

To Milfred Valentine: I will forever be grateful for your belief in me and for providing me with an opportunity that truly started my path to adulthood. You were an amazing music director and an even more amazing role model and human being. Thank you.

To Judy Cooper: Thank you for believing in me when I was just twenty-four. In the time we worked together, you taught me more about employee management than I could have possibly learned anywhere else. Be direct but kind. Provide guidance but hold people accountable. Be a boss first but do not hesitate to extend the branch of friendship. I am so lucky to have had you in my life, and I love that we are still in touch thirty-five years later!

To Barry O'Brien: You left us far too early, but I am grateful for the opportunity you gave me and the mentoring you provided. Watching you lead the company gave me foresight into the manager, leader, and mentor I wanted to be.

To Steve Schulman: You always believed in me and were there when I needed you. You were central in teaching me that quality patient care and capitalism could coexist. Thank you for the fun times, the tough times, and all the life lessons.

To Jason Potts: I can still remember our first meeting to discuss investment strategies and ultimately bonding over our growing families. Thank you for being there for me and my family as our financial advisor but even more as our friend. I appreciate all you do. To my Tiger 21 Family, both past and present: You have been and continue to be some of the most impactful people I know. I am so honored to share this comradery as we continue to grow as friends, entrepreneurs, and philanthropists.

To Budd, Janet, Doris, Randi, Rob, Scott, Chris, and the rest of the Fischer/Feder family: Thank you for accepting me into your lives, and thank you for your continued love and support. Although she left us far too soon, your daughter/sister, Marcia Fischer Webb, will always be in my heart and in my thoughts. She was such an amazing partner in every sense of the word. Without her support and love, I would not have achieved my dreams. I will never let her legacy be forgotten. Thank you from the deepest depths of my heart.

To my many friends, business partners, coworkers, allies, and those of you who represent all these: Thank you for being part of this journey. Each of you, in your own way, has been such a positive force in my life. We have weathered many storms together, but all that pales when I think of the fun ride we have had over the past forty years. I have always been humbled by your level of caring and support and cannot wait to see what the next chapter of our lives has in store for all of us.

To my children, Elizabeth, Maxwell, Joseph, Kristen, and Carly, as well as your significant others and my grandchildren: You will forever be my beacon of light and the reason I will continue to focus on our future. I am so proud of each and every one of you, and I am so looking forward to watching you pursue your dreams. Work hard. Play hard. Respect and care for each other. Help those in need. You got this. I know it.

And finally, to my beautiful wife, Catherine Lynne: I have said it many times, and I will continue to shout it from the hills: In my darkest hour, God sent me an angel. He sent me Catherine Lynne O'Keefe. Brought together by circumstances beyond our control, I am so thankful that I found you. Your love for my family is equaled only by my love for yours. Your acceptance of my past is one of the many building blocks that you have brought to our relationship, and there is no one else on this planet I would rather continue my life with than you. I am grateful to God every day for having you in my life. I love you with all that I am and all that I will ever be.

WHY CAN'T THE WEBBS BE THE NEXT ROCKEFELLERS?

This is the American dream in a nutshell: You come from nothing, but in a land of opportunity, the person with the guts and determination to make something of themselves rises up and creates a fortune out of dust. It's a story you've heard a million times before, and it's the most American story imaginable. More American even than cowboys and baseball. Every bit as American as apple pie.

If you had looked at the odds when I was born, you would not have bet on me getting to the point where I spend my days pondering the pitfalls of generational wealth. I was born to teenage parents in Laurel, Mississippi. Where I come from, there are limited opportunities—a job at the Masonite plant, at Howard Industries making electrical transformers, at Sanderson Farms, or maybe working offshore. If you were ambitious, maybe junior college. The rich kids got to go to Ole Miss. Don't take that observation as a judgment. Those

1

are the people I come from, and I love them more than anything. But through sheer luck, determination, and bullheaded resilience, I managed to get out of the cycle of low expectations that trapped so many people I knew, and so many of them were just like me.

I didn't have a big plan. It's not like I used to stay up all night reading business books and designing schemes. I wasn't a scholar, and I wasn't a prodigy or some touched-by-God brainiac. In other words, I wasn't born special. And I don't believe I am today. But I do know how hard I worked to get to where I am, and I do know how building wealth has given my immediate family an incredible opportunity to contribute to our larger family, to our friends, and to people in need.

It's not about the money. Well, it is, but it's not entirely about the money. I don't apologize for being a capitalist. I won't apologize for working hard in the pursuit of wealth. Why should I? You're an idiot if you're a rich guy who tries to deny that he's rich, and for the first generation, he'd have to be a liar or a fool to claim he wasn't driven by the pursuit of wealth. I may be a dumb redneck, but I am not a liar or a fool.

The money makes our lives different from most, but it also allows us to think beyond the money. We can take the money we have and use it to make more money through a family business. We can use it to serve people in need. We can use it to change the fortunes of other families in need. I may have worked my tail off to get where I am, but I didn't do it alone; there were people along the way who recognized something in me that I didn't recognize in myself and who did what they could to help me change my life.

Changing fate, my perceived pathway at birth, is an important idea to me. That was my goal, the thing that kept me going when the work was hard and the hours were long. It was the desire to change my family's fate for the long haul that got me back up every time I was knocked down. Now my wife, Cathy, our five kids, and I have the chance to help other people change their destiny in life through our philanthropic efforts.

My work has changed a great deal over the last few years. I don't run companies the way I used to, as CEO or COO. I'm an investor, an adviser, and a chairman—things a person can only do if they've been through hell and come out on top. Today I work *on* the business rather than *in* the business, which gives me the time to focus on what matters most—my family and our future.

In the chapters that follow, you will learn about my story—how a small-town kid living in near poverty found his way into the medical imaging field. You'll read about how I was held at gunpoint by the Sandinistas and about how I met people who changed my life with their guidance, love, and strength. You'll learn about amazing wins and devastating losses, about sin and redemption, about recovery and forward momentum.

When you finish the last page, you will be tempted to think that you have reached the end of the story—a story that, apart from the particulars, seems a lot like some of the others you've heard before.

But for my family and me—my beautiful family brought together by love and circumstances both happy and heartbreaking—it is still just the beginning. When you've been through what we've been through, you can't let the story end where this book ends. You have to keep thinking about the future and doing everything you can to make sure that it's a future worthy of the journey, a journey defined not by obstacles but by wholehearted belief and dedication to one simple question: Why not?

Most importantly, in this book you will learn the benefit and advantage of resilience. If I can claim any single attribute that has been the key to the success I've had, it is resilience. If I can pass on anything to our children and to the generations that follow, it's a resilient spirit, bolstered by family and dedicated to changing the fate of families—ours and others'.

Resilience isn't just about getting back up. Any fool can get back up when they've been knocked down. What other choice do you have, besides staying down in the gutter? A resilient person never considers staying down. Getting back up is an instinct, like breathing or blinking. Resilient people never take their eyes off where they're going, even when they get knocked down. They don't take it easy; they don't retire. They refocus.

Wealth helps you do that, but it's a means, not an end. When wealth is the only thing that defines a family, they fall apart nine times out of ten, and with them goes the money. But a family built on love, compassion, communication, and resilience might just end up changing the world. That's the family I want our family to be and why I spend so much time thinking about what I can do to make it happen. It's why I ask myself, *Why can't the Webbs be the next Rockefellers? Why not us?*

CHAPTER ONE

WHERE THE HECK IS LAUREL, MISSISSIPPI?

Resilience: When you are born in a small town in Mississippi, where opportunities are few and less is expected, you must find your motivation from within. Despite setbacks, you must remain resilient and focused on the future that you dream of for yourself.

You have probably never heard of Laurel. No one would blame you. It's a cute, small town in the southeast part of Mississippi. It has about twenty thousand people and lots of parks but not much else. The town is surrounded by smaller communities: Glade, Shady Grove, Ellisville, Tuckers Crossing, and Lake Bogue Homa. The Masonite plant was the big employer when I was born, and I grew up thinking I'd be working there too. If not there, it probably would have been Sanderson Farms (chickens) or offshore on an oil platform.

There are a few notable people who've come from Laurel. The actress Parker Posey, the opera singer Leontyne Price, and the NFL running back Clinton Portis, along with a few other football players. After I was grown and left town, Lance Bass, from the 1990s boy band NSYNC, was born and raised in Laurel. But other than that, Laurel is and has always been an out-of-the-way place full of nice people living in their own little world. There is nothing wrong with that, and I have great memories, but that narrow life was not for me. There's a downtown business district built around the historic courthouse that is straight out of a John Grisham book. Big shade trees cover the small streets like umbrellas, and even now the city is full of parks. A lot has changed in the nearly six decades since I was born there, but just as much has stayed the same. You don't need to know Laurel to understand it. It's a small town in the heart of the Old South, where reputations carry currency and everybody knows too much about everybody else.

This is the downtown Laurel that I remember as a kid.

I was born in Laurel, the product of two high schoolers who fell in love a little too early. They were just kids, teenagers who didn't know much about the world beyond their home lives and inner needs. It was the late 1950s, and the town was divided, as it always had been. The rich white families lived up on Bay Springs Road. The poor African American families lived on the other side of the tracks. My parents were neither black nor rich, and they did right be me and each other, getting married and becoming part of the third group in town—the poor working whites just trying to get by and put food on the table.

This was the Jim Crowe South, but although segregation was the norm, I was never raised with hate in my life or in my heart. My first best friend in grammar school, Alvin, was African American. The best teacher I ever had, Miss Love, was African American. I used to tell my parents, "I love Miss Love." Unlike many of the other teachers I had, she actually cared about us as students and as human beings. She was a big influence in my life.

There were natural divides among the three groups and even more so after the schools were desegregated—shortly after which a brand-new, expensive private school popped up in a little town just north of Laurel, where the parents on Bay Springs Road, who weren't too excited about the progress of desegregation, sent their kids.

The churches followed the divide as well. First Baptist Church was for the wealthy families. First Methodist was for the next group. We went to the Second Avenue Baptist Church and had about four hundred members, with most being the white working class. The African American families in town went to their own church. Nowhere were social and economic divides in Laurel more apparent than in church circles. Having an African American best friend may have gotten me talked about among the other white families in our part of town, a fact I accepted, but I would never have dreamed of inviting him to church or going to his.

My parents didn't have much to give me other than love. My dad worked for a local electrician company, as an apprentice, for fifty cents an hour, sixty hours a week. We lived in a little white house next to the shop, which I think the owner, Mr. Blackledge, rented to my folks on the cheap because he felt for a couple of teenagers trying to start their lives as a family. I spent a lot of time with my mom, and one of my earliest childhood memories is of a drawing she made of an octopus and a swan, which hung over the bathtub. She did it for me, to take care of me. Mom was always taking care of people when I was a kid. She still does to this day.

My mom with me and my brother, circa 1964.

We spent a lot of time at church. There were Sunday services and Sunday School, of course, and I remember Sunday mornings being very Bible focused. It was about God's Word and only the Word. We'd go back on Sunday evenings for another service, which was meant to be more educational. It was about applying the Word to your life. Wednesday evenings we went to prayer meetings, and there was usually a potluck dinner once a month. Thursday night was choir practice, which was also sometimes scheduled for the time between Sunday services. When I was older, I'd spend the other days at the church rec center playing basketball and ping-pong and whatever else was around. Church was religion, but it was also the social glue that held our community together. I liked being there. I liked being around the people in our community, among other people and other families like ours.

The church choir was an important part of my childhood, and the director, Milfred Valentine, was one of the people who set me on my path. I remember tossing a football around with some other kids outside the church one day when Milfred came up to us and asked for the ball. We snickered at the thought of our choir director being able to hold the ball, let alone throw it. But we were set straight when he fired a perfect spiral like it was no big deal. It turned out that in addition to leading our church choir and teaching music at Jones County Junior College, Milfred was also an All-Conference high school football quarterback. I learned right there not to make assumptions about people and that you can be into the arts and also be athletic. When I was young, choir was something to look forward to, just like baseball games and Scout outings. Even when I got to high school and had given up sports in favor of work, partying, and chasing girls, I remained in the choir. I'm glad I did, too, because Milfred offered me a half scholarship to the junior college, and all I had to do was sing in the choir. Without him, I might never have pursued higher education, and I might still think of people as being capable of only one thing in their lives. He was another big influence.

There was a large courthouse on the center square and a shopping district with a Woolworths, JCPenney, Rexall Drugstore, some men's clothing stores, Burton's Jewelry, and a movie theater that I remember paying a nickel to get into when I was young. There was a store, Fine Brothers Madison, that only the families on Bay Springs Road could afford. I sneaked into it a few times and can still remember the mannequins in fur coats. My mom would work seasonal shifts at the local Sears & Roebuck store to pay for layaway Christmas gifts that my parents bought for my two brothers and me.

Five generations in my family.

The Masonite factory, the chicken farms, and the oil fields put food on a lot of tables in Laurel, but none of my family worked at those places. My dad's parents—Lottie Mae and Harold Webb—owned a little corner store called Webb's Stop & Shop. Lottie was a hard worker at the store every day. Harold was a fireman and one of the influences in my life. Harold's mom, my great-grandmother, Grannie, was one of the most loving women I have ever met. She was the matriarch of the Webbs. You went to Lottie Mae for a popsicle. You went to Grannie for a hug and stewed potatoes and cornbread, which is my favorite meal to this day.

My mom's family, the Logans, were also in town and in our lives. AC Logan was my papaw, and I don't know that there was a nicer man in town. He was also the only person I knew at the time with an education. He was a lab and X-ray tech at one of the local hospitals. I used to hang out with him at the hospital and watch him work. He also had a TV repair business in his garage. As a child, we got our first few TVs from him so that we could watch WDAM, Channel 7, the only TV station available. *The Three Stooges* and *Popeye* dominated the early mornings, and Perry Como and Andy Williams held our attention at night. My papaw was a huge influence on me and one of the reasons I initially followed his career. My mom's mother was Kitty, and she was a tough one. She was the quickest to reach for the belt or switch to "teach us a lesson." Because she did not have a job, we spent a fair bit of time with her. I have good memories of her cooking and crafting but also some not so good memories of her version of punishment. She was tough on me, tough on my mom, tough on my dad, tough on my papaw. Just tough.

When I was two, we moved out of that little white house next to the electrician shop where my dad worked to our new place at 2128

Second Avenue. My parents paid $9,000 for the house, and I have memories of them struggling to make their mortgage. It was about this time when my brother Ronney was born. My parents didn't give him a middle name, and later in life, he would petition the court to add "Joe" to his birth records. He wanted a *J* in his name like the rest of us. Ronney and I were really good buddies but contentious just the same. We palled around and had a lot of fun, but two of the four best fights I've ever had in my life were with Ronney. We always kissed and made up.

By the time I was eight, my dad had started working for the county electricity company as a lineman and things had gotten a little better. My brother Chris was born that year and revealed himself to be a very sweet, loving boy from the beginning. He was also a good athlete and went on to pitch in college before finding his true calling—helping others through counseling and service. Both he and Ronney grew up to be Southern Baptist preachers.

Between my parents and grandparents, there were always presents under the Christmas tree and food on the table, but I always wanted more. I'll cover my work life in the next few chapters, but suffice it to say that my world in those early years was defined by four things: the neighborhood, church, work, and school. I don't know whether my parents saw potential in me or if they didn't know any better, but I started first grade when I was five. I was already a relatively small kid, but being in a class of thirty kids, all of whom were at least a year or two older than me, might have had something to do with my immediate disinterest in school. Our teacher, Miss Odem, used to hit us on the palm of our hand with a ruler when we acted out, and even though I realized I was too young to be in school, I knew better than to complain too much. School wasn't meant to be fun. It was meant to toughen me up.

We had a little gang in the neighborhood, the Second Avenue Raiders. We'd sneak out at night and go on adventures, play a lot of baseball, and just generally run around the neighborhood like we owned the place. I felt a level of comfort with those guys that I never felt at school. Some of us played Little League baseball together on a team started by my dad and my papaw. I started off as a bat boy but eventually made it to the Little League Cubs and played for other teams all the way through my sophomore year in high school.

Sports was the basis of the relationship that I had with my dad. I spent a lot of time with Mom and we were close, but as I look back, I realize that I probably had a better relationship with my dad than my friends had with theirs or that even my brothers had with him. He was a good athlete when he was in school, and Chris, who pitched in the College World Series, probably got his talent from Dad. I've wondered more than once what would have happened to his life if I hadn't come along.

My dad and I, just chillin'.

I don't think he or Mom were looking for a long-term relationship when they got together. Mom had a rough time growing up, and I think Dad treated her well, a gift that she craved. Dad was probably just like any other teenage boy, drawn by instincts as old as time. They fought a lot when I was young, but I don't remember either one of them ever showing resentment toward or blaming me for their lot in life. We were far from a perfect family, but we made it through, and I have always admired my parents for what they did to provide for my brothers and me. It might not have been a picturesque situation, but there was a lot to be proud of, particularly how my parents demonstrated resilience in their lives.

When I was bumbling my way through high school, my mom, who had always been a caregiver, decided to go back to school. She picked up a student loan for $525 per quarter and studied nursing at the local junior college for the first two years, then finished her degree at the University of Southern Mississippi. I had never thought too much about college, but seeing Mom do it made me think it was possible. My dad never went to college, but it was important to him that I go. I remember him telling me, "I want you to go to college so you don't have to work for a living." I didn't understand what he meant and was kind of disappointed because I wanted to work for him in the electrical business. Then one day in 2001, it finally made sense to me. I was driving in Dallas through a brutal winter storm, and while stuck on an overpass, I looked up to see a lineman working on a power line in the freezing dark. Boom—I got it. That's what Dad meant by working for a living. He wanted more for my brothers and me and for himself too.

But wanting more doesn't always mean achieving it. When I was a senior in high school, my dad started an HVAC company. For the first time in his life, he was working for himself and finding success. But then, one day, the IRS showed up at the door and took just about everything he had. His accountant had been skimming and not paying the bills, and in the blink of an eye, everything my dad had built was gone and he was saddled with debt. He could have quit right there. God knows there were people in our neighborhood who would have done just that, but if Chris got Dad's throwing arm, I was blessed with his resilience. He rebounded and paid off every last cent, which nearly killed him, but it is one of the things he did in life that impressed me the most. He was responsible and he was resilient.

When I think back to my youth in Laurel, I can see the building blocks of the person I eventually became. I don't remember learning that much in school, but that doesn't mean I didn't learn in my youth. I inherited nothing monetary from my relatives and friends, but I abso-lutely got some of their traits. I got my grandparents' entrepreneurial spirit and my mom's instinct to take care of people. I got my dad's work ethic and resilience in the face of failure. I got my sense of community from church. I learned bravery in the face of stupidity from Alvin and Miss Love and all the African American families who crossed the segregation lines. From the rich parents who would rather start a school of their own than let their kids go to school with Alvin or learn from Miss Love, I learned the wrong way to be successful. I learned that tragedy can influence you without defining you and that life doesn't double back to help you out.

You have to do it for yourself.

I DON'T REMEMBER LEARNING THAT MUCH IN SCHOOL, BUT THAT DOESN'T MEAN I DIDN'T LEARN IN MY YOUTH.

REDNECK RECAP

Family and outside influences start at an early age.
Embrace them. Learn from them. Challenge yourself.

CHAPTER TWO

POTHOLDERS AND BLOOD ON A PILLOW

*Resilience: Most of us don't know from an early age exactly
what we want to do. Many will take the wrong path time and
again until they find their true calling. Those small failures
build resilience and the temperament for eventual success.*

The potholders were going for five cents apiece, and they looked easy enough to make. I was about five years old and attending a church-sponsored bazaar, where folks were selling everything from vegetables to old clothes to handmade items. It was then, on the front lawn of the Second Avenue Baptist Church, when I had my first business idea: learn how to make potholders and sell a lot of them.

Despite being a mediocre student, I wasn't dumb. I understood the connection between opportunity, effort, and outcome from a very early age. This was in no small part because I couldn't rely on other people to get me the things I wanted, and I always wanted more—things, sure, but also freedom and opportunity. I remember knowing that if there was something extra I wanted, I had to get it for myself. That's why the potholders stuck out to me. They looked uncomplicated but could be made flashy, and everyone seemed to be buying them. My mom taught me the basics of weaving a potholder, and I eventually learned how to make patterns and even words in the designs. Our church would have these bazaars, potluck dinners, and yard and craft sales. Some of the things were junk and didn't get bought. Some things were expensive and were a more considered purchase. But everyone seemed to be buying those potholders and particularly from a kid. Over the course of three years, I made and sold a ton of them.

How do I know that I sold a boatload? Because I saved the money and used it to buy a lawn mower when I was eight years old—and the James Webb Lawn Service was born. I mowed lawns, pulled weeds, and raked leaves. I walked door-to-door and made my pitch to neighbors who were either impressed by my entrepreneurial spirit or too tired to mow their own lawns. I did that until the year I turned twelve, at which time I transformed my lawn-mowing income into my next business opportunity. I bought a Schwinn bicycle—the most badass purchase and possession of my young life—and went down to the local newspaper office to sign up for a delivery route.

Unlike mowing lawns, which was something I did mostly by myself unless my dad was helping me with repairs or my brother was joining me to rake or mow, the paper route was more of a family affair. I have fond memories of sitting with my mom or my brothers or my grandparents, rolling up the papers, and loading up my satchel before heading out on my run. I collected the subscription money and learned a lot of discipline on the cold and rainy days when I would rather stay in bed than get on my bike and cover my early-morning route.

When I was thirteen years old, I bought my first car. Yep, thirteen. It was a Plymouth station wagon that I took off my parents' hands for the whopping sum of fifty dollars. I wasn't old enough to get a driver's license, of course, but that didn't mean I couldn't drive. Maybe it was a sign of the trust my parents had in me or just a sign of the times, but I used to drive my brother Ronney to grammar school before parking a few blocks away from the middle school and walking the rest of the way. And for a very short time, I continued my paper route throwing newspapers from my car. Delivering papers was a lot more fun and exciting when I did it from my own car. Grab a rolled-up newspaper, hang it out the driver's side window, throw it over the car's roof, and land it on the porch. I missed only a few times and once broke a window! I also don't remember ever getting caught driving underage, but if I had been, I doubt I would have been in too much trouble with my parents. Mom, who had three boys driving her crazy at home, and Dad, who worked a lot, probably liked the fact that their oldest boy was seeking and gaining independence. The young parents needed their oldest to make his own way, and I always remember them supporting that concept.

The paper route and mowing lawns were the perfect jobs for me. I didn't really answer to anyone—other than the man at the newspaper office who delivered my papers and took the money I collected—and I could make money without sacrificing too much of my childhood. I could still run around with the Second Avenue Raiders, play baseball, take karate classes at the YMCA, and chase girls while having some money in my pocket and my sights set on my next goal. I didn't mind working either. I liked it. I liked to be busy. Idle hands and all that, or maybe it was the precursor of what today would be diagnosed as ADHD. If I hadn't been working, I probably would have gotten into a lot more trouble than I did. The Second Avenue Raiders were always playing pranks on people. If I hadn't had work to do and money to make, I probably would have taken one of those pranks too far and done some real damage.

Working at a young age and seeing my family work developed "muscles" in me that I worry may be lost for my own kids if I'm not careful. I worked out of a necessity manifested in a couple of forms—the monetary but also the activity. I remember seeing my first television at my grandparents' house. I was born too early for video games, and the kinds of distractions kids have today were not even pipe dreams back then. All we had were sports, clubs (I was a Scout), church, and work to keep us out of trouble. Work came with the added bonus of a paycheck.

My first look at entrepreneurship. My grandparents, Harold and Lottie Webb, opened a small food vending business.

An early adoption of work habits combined with a lukewarm (at best) interest in school drew my attention to the DECA program when I entered high school. At that time DECA stood for the Distributive Education Clubs of America. It was essentially a work study. We'd get out of school every day at 1:00 p.m. to go to work in a local business or industry for real-world learning. Anything to get me out of school sounded good, plus, again, there was the opportunity to get paid. I took a job working for MCB Business Services in Laurel, which is probably best described as a precursor to Kinko's printing services. I made paper pads and copies (mimeographs), designed flyers, took photographs, and delivered products all over town. Eventually, I even learned to operate the printing presses and at one point was the pressman for that small company. It was hard work and hot down in the windowless basement workroom.

I worked for that company all the way through high school and stayed on after I graduated. I didn't know what I wanted to do. Heading off to Ole Miss or Mississippi State wasn't in the cards. That was for the rich kids, and anyway, I wasn't sure I had the grades to get in. Plus, I'd worked enough to know that spending a lot for college when you didn't know what you wanted to do was a waste of both time and money. My parents didn't pressure me, other than to indicate that it was time to move. My mom had gone back to school and was still going when I was ready to graduate high school. Dad hoped I'd go to college so that I wouldn't have to work for a living. But I wasn't convinced that college was for me. I considered the oil fields. And I considered the Masonite plant. It was only when the church choir director, Milfred Valentine, offered me a half scholarship to Jones County Junior College to sing in the choir that I thought perhaps I could go to college. I don't think the scholarship was official. I suspect he might have paid for it out of his own pocket, which is why he remains, to this day, one of a handful of people who changed my life. He was a truly good man whom I was blessed to have in my life.

I decided to enroll for the fall quarter, but then, in August of that year, a couple of things happened that, like Milfred's scholarship, changed the direction of my life. The first was that my high school girlfriend dumped me. She was heading off to college and didn't think a long-distance romance would work. Either that or she wanted more than she thought I was willing to give. In retrospect, I don't think I was ready to marry her, but the example of early marriage had been set by my folks and the thought had probably crossed my mind. She made the decision for me when she moved on, leaving me with even less direction than I'd had before.

It probably wasn't the next day, but it was close to that when I woke up and found a pool of blood on my pillow. I didn't think much of it that day. I just cleaned it up and moved on. But then it happened again the next day—and the day after that and the day after that—for close to six weeks, which is when I got scared enough to ask for help.

While growing up, I had earaches. Nothing terrible but fairly regularly. The only other health scare I ever had was when I was five years old, swinging on the swing set my dad had put up in the backyard and singing "Jesus Loves Me." I fell off the swing and bit my tongue almost completely off. My parents took me to the emergency room, and the doctors said they could sew it back on, but they couldn't use pain medication. They tied me to the table and stitched it back together before sending me home. By the time we got back to the house, the stitches had come loose, and we turned around and went back to the ER to do it all over again. That one lasted about a day, so we went back to the hospital for a third time. Tied down, no pain medicine. Stitched through and through my tongue. This time it worked.

I don't think you need to be a psychologist to make the connection between my hesitation to see a doctor about the blood coming out of my ears and that early experience of having my tongue sewn on without so much as a local anesthetic three times in two days. So believe me, things were pretty bad for me to ask to be taken to the ER.

The summer after high school, I started waking up each morning with blood on my pillow. I kept ignoring it until it knocked me down and out. I was diagnosed with encephalitis, an inflammation of the lining of the brain that was potentially fatal. It was determined to have been brought on by tumors in my inner ears, called cholesteatomas. These benign fatty tumors were made of cholesterol, and although they weren't cancer, the acid from the cholesterol had eaten through the bones in my inner ears, through the lining of my skull, and into my brain. I spent three weeks in the hospital surviving and recovering. The doctors told me I had probably had the growths for a while and they may have been the source of some of those regular earaches. They also told me I was lucky it didn't get worse and kill me.

The incident on the swing set had left me with a lifelong scar across my tongue. This incident left me with hearing loss, particularly in my left ear, and forced me to delay my enrollment at Jones County Junior College. For the first time since I was five years old, I wasn't going to school in the fall, and the recovery left me sitting on the couch for weeks watching the only channel our TV received. I learned to love soap operas, and even though I tried, it was the least productive period in my work life.

The silver lining in all this was that missing the first quarter of college got me pretty excited about the prospect of going to school. I didn't know what I wanted to do and took basic courses while working during the off hours. I thought about maybe becoming a choir director, such was the influence Milfred Valentine had on my life. Then one day I walked into the science building and saw a mimeographed flyer—the same kind I'd made a thousand times in the basement print shop—advertising an X-ray tech program offered through the county hospital, with the contact information for a woman named Liz Bush.

Papaw Logan, my mom's dad, ran the lab at a small hospital, and I reached out to him to ask about the program and to see if he could introduce me to Liz Bush. He did indeed know her and made arrangements for me to interview to be a part of the program, which was affiliated with Jones County Junior College and offered credits that could be transferred there or to a four-year college. Even now, I realize the luck involved in seeing that flyer. Had I enrolled in the first quarter as planned, I might never have been in the science building that day. It wasn't like I had an interest in medicine before then. In fact, it only caught my eye because the flyer looked like one I had made at work and because the X-ray technician sounded somewhat related to what Papaw Logan did, and he and I were very close. Had he not known about the program or Liz Bush, I may not have pursued it any further.

The last picture of me before X-ray tech school and a haircut.

I believe in hard work. I believe in taking risks. I believe in failure and in the resilience needed to overcome it. But I believe in dumb luck, too, and seeing that flyer that day was one of the luckiest moments of my life.

If Milfred Valentine remains a force in my life for his kindness and empathy and for opening my mind, Liz Bush remains for the way she kicked my ass. She was tough, the kind of taskmaster who defines theory X. She ran the program with an iron fist and a titanium will, which sounds terrible, but it was exactly what an aimless, partying eighteen-year-old needed. And despite that ass kicking, over

My Papaw Logan. He was a big influence in my life and helped guide me to X-ray tech school.

The radiology program was tough. There were times when it got to be too much, and I tried to leave. A lot of people quit, but for some reason, Liz Bush wouldn't let me. One time, I walked out of the X-ray room and told her I was done. Another kind of person might have looked at me and said something encouraging or told me to think about my future, but not Liz. She smacked me on the back, yelled, "Get your ass back in there," and made it clear that failure was not an option. It reminded me of Miss Odem hitting us with rulers in first grade, and I managed to stick with it. I barely passed the school parts, but when it came time to take the ARRT, the test that qualifies X-ray technicians for the national registry, I got the second-highest score in the state. Liz Bush, like Milfred Valentine, had seen something in me that I could not recognize in myself.

Between the program and my time moonlighting, I spent a lot of time in hospitals those couple of years. I liked the work, but there was something keeping me from diving in professionally when I finished my two-year degree. Or, more accurately, there was someone who caught my eye and made me think about bigger things. It didn't matter which hospital I was in or which floor I was working on; there were plenty of people in white coats and uniforms, but there was only ever one guy in a suit, and a really nice one at that. I asked another tech about the guy in the suit, and he told me that the man was the Kodak sales rep. The company was the biggest name in medical tech at the time, and the cut of the man's suit showed it. He looked successful and powerful. He looked like his life was full of more money and excitement than that of the people in the lab, and I made a decision right then and there: I was going to get a four-year degree and become that guy.

REDNECK RECAP

Life is a journey. You may not know your exact path, but begin defining your direction early. Focus on the next step.

CHAPTER THREE

TAKING LEAPS AND CHOOSING NEW LANDINGS

Resilience: When life presents you with opportunities, you can stay the course—or lift your head to seek farther horizons, taking risk and overcoming obstacles, with your eye on the prize of your own choosing.

I t's amazing how much power we put in a little piece of paper. Coming out of Jones County Junior College, I knew I had to go back to school if I was going to change the direction I was headed, and I needed a little piece of paper—a four-year degree. I knew I was smart enough for college, but my first impression of school established back in first grade hadn't changed much in the intervening years: go to class, do the work, give me my diploma. I had bigger fish to fry.

Regina made it better, though. We'd met while I was studying in the tech program. She was working on a nursing degree, and I thought she was funny and cute. I wanted to get to know her better. I was so sure—and so stupid and so cocky—that during a party, I stole a deposit slip from her purse when she wasn't looking, just to get her phone number. When I got home from the party, I realized I'd lost the slip and so I reached out to my guardian angel and choir director Milfred Valentine for help. He taught at Jones County Junior College and thus had access to student schedules. I told him my problem, and he told me what class she would be in at what time. When the time came, I marched right into her class and asked her out.

I don't know how to describe our relationship other than that it was a bit of a whirlwind romance. We were engaged within nine months, and by the time I was ready to finish my degree, we were married and living in a special dorm for married couples. She was going to Southern Miss, and I was studying at nearby William Carey College. I use the word *studying* lightly because I was mostly working my ass off. Classes were from eight to noon every day and then I worked a two-to-ten night shift at the hospital, ten days on followed by four days off. Most nights, I drove the thirty miles home, passed out, and then got up at six the next morning to do it all over again.

I was newly married, and my schedule made it impossible to have any kind of regular job to help support my wife and me. But, if there's anything I've learned in my life that's worth passing on to my children, it's that resilient people find a way of working things out. They don't sit around and complain and hope that their complaining leads to results. They roll up their sleeves and make something of a bad situation. My third business was born out of necessity, just like the potholders and the lawn mowing before it.

On my four days off from my night shift job in Laurel, I set up a little company providing X-ray technician services to rural hospitals all over central and south Mississippi. A lot of smaller hospitals couldn't afford to keep someone on staff for weekends or overnight, and I saw an opportunity. For $250 and a bed to sleep in, I would work from Friday night to Sunday night, forty-eight hours straight, doing X-rays and other services and providing an extra set of hands in the ER. I even helped some of my classmates get similar gigs to help support themselves, and after eighteen months, I managed to graduate from William Carey College with my bachelor's degree. My original idea had been to be the Kodak man, but another opportunity came calling, and it was too good—and strange—to pass up.

Immediately before my graduation and at twenty-two years of age, I was named the director of education of the Jones County Junior College X-Ray Technician Program. The very same program I had completed eighteen months earlier under the firm-handed leadership of Liz Bush was now mine to run. I had fifteen students, all around my age and some I had even gone to high school with. Over the next eighteen months, I learned some lessons I still carry with me today. I found that I loved to teach. I enjoyed guiding and mentoring students and realized just how much I liked to be the center of attention—to be listened to and followed. I had respected Liz Bush's theory X management style—even if I didn't appreciate it—and found myself trying to be like her. I realized, however, that I preferred a more patient and inclusive style. Managing those students was like captaining a ship full of sailors your own age who had only slightly less experience than you. If I had come in with a strong hand and a sharp tongue, I might have found myself facing a mutiny. Still, I tried to emulate Liz's strength and certainty, even if my edges were slightly less sharp.

*Me with three of my students. We had won an award
from the State Radiology Society.*

Instead of just working, as I had my whole life, I now found myself leading and even became involved in a movement to shift hospital-based tech programs out of the hospital and into universities. This was near and dear to my heart, given my aversion to the forced labor aspect of the hospital-based program I had completed. I became the local lead of a national movement that ended up demanding that the accrediting society outlaw the fruitless practice of uncompensated student labor. Students may not get a paycheck, but they would get college credit, which had a monetary value of its own. They would also receive a better education and a more manageable lifestyle.

I was proud to be a part of that movement, and although I enjoyed teaching, I found myself feeling restless. Regina and I were renting a little house in Laurel, and I remember sitting on the couch one afternoon, sipping a Miller Pony beer and looking around, asking myself what I wanted to do next. I'd spent enough time in school to know that I liked teaching but didn't want to do it for the rest of my life. The fact that I made $8.36 per hour was cool … but not cool enough. I was ambitious, and I wanted many things. I'd spent enough time in hospitals to know that I could make a decent living as a tech but that I could make a much better one in administration. In order to be a hospital administrator, I would need a master's degree. I decided in that moment to head back to school. The only question was where.

Regina had family in Dallas, but Atlanta was a logical place for small-town folks with bigger aspirations to go. I pulled out a coin and flipped it. Heads we go to Dallas, tails we go to Atlanta. Heads won. I turned in my resignation the next day. Two weeks later I loaded up a pickup truck and a bass boat, and Regina and I were on our way to Texas.

We spent the first few nights sleeping in the truck but eventually moved into a rental house with Regina's sister in Duncanville, on the southwest side of Dallas. I got a job as an X-ray tech and enrolled in the MBA program at the University of Texas at Arlington while Regina worked as a nurse. It wasn't a defining time in my life, but like so many things I have done, it led to something that would be. I wasn't particularly happy. Work was fine, but I didn't really feel comfortable at UTA, and living with Regina's sister was not going well. I got antsy. I knew I needed a change, which is why, six months into our new life, I was looking in the newspaper when I noticed an advertisement for a chief technologist position at Lewisville Memorial Hospital and decided to apply.

At age twenty-four, I probably wasn't the most qualified person for the position, but if I waited to be qualified to try something, I would have never left Laurel. I have met many people—in business and in life—who seem to trust in the philosophy that your next move should be the one for which you're already prepared. I disagree. I believe in pursuing your desired path regardless of your level of preparation. Be decisive. Be confident in the fact that if you're smart and focused, you'll learn faster when you're in over your head or out of your depth. I have had people tell me that I'm a risk-taker, but it hardly ever feels like a risk. So the thought that I might be too young or too underqualified or too anything to apply for that position never entered my mind. Instead, I trusted my gut, trusted my brain, and trusted myself enough to not get in my own way.

> **BE CONFIDENT IN THE FACT THAT IF YOU'RE SMART AND FOCUSED, YOU'LL LEARN FASTER WHEN YOU'RE IN OVER YOUR HEAD OR OUT OF YOUR DEPTH.**

And it worked.

I got the job, which was on the exact opposite end of Dallas from where we lived and where I went to school. I commuted back and forth, an hour each way, until the end of my school term and then packed up and moved us to our new life in Lewisville, Texas.

I have reached an age now when I can look back and recognize the decisions and people who have steered my life's course. I've mentioned a few of them already, but Judy Cooper belongs on the Mount Rushmore of people who have changed me. She was the director of radiology at Lewisville Hospital, which made her my boss, but she was unlike any boss I had ever had before.

Judy Cooper opened my eyes to the magic powers of contingency management. Manage the situation; don't rule it. Care for your people; don't set them up for failure. Hold them accountable; don't be a dictator. And above all things, you don't have to be an asshole to be effective. Her style was like a breath of clean morning air, and I loved her for it right away. I decided I could work for her for the rest of my life, but that was not to be the case. Just three months after I arrived in Lewisville, Judy resigned her position and, in a parting move that still blows my mind today, recommended me for her job.

Nine months after I had sat on that couch, sipping a beer and wishing for a change, I became the youngest director of radiology in the United States. I had moved to Duncanville where I was an X-ray tech and then moved to Lewisville. I started an MBA program at UT Arlington and dropped out, then enrolled in a master of health administration program at the University of North Texas. I was a chief technologist and then department director, and I even served on the hospital Executive Committee. For four years, my life moved pretty consistently. I worked from eight to five, took classes two to four nights a week, developed a bunch of friendships, and became a father to my wonderful daughter, Elizabeth Jayne.

And that's a story unto itself. Regina was full-blown pregnant and ready to give birth, but we went out for some Cajun fried chicken and attended a party at someone's house. When we got home, I playfully patted her butt, and boom, her water broke. It was Katy bar the door as we hustled to the hospital. At that time, we checked in through the emergency room before being admitted upstairs to the maternity area. While in the ER, I suddenly got sick and had to run to the bathroom to throw up. Now, remember, I worked at that hospital, so I immediately got grief for not being able to handle the situation. But the vomiting didn't stop, so they put me in one of the ER rooms and took Regina up to maternity. I got sicker, to the point that my blood pressure bottomed out and more doctors were brought in to figure out what was going on with me. Eventually, with IVs attached to my arms, they moved me to one of the four VIP rooms in the hospital. I proceeded to flood the room with my vomit. They moved me to the second VIP room, where I also baptized it with my body fluids.

Finally, in the third VIP room, I passed out. A male nurse friend of mine woke me up, handed me the phone, and I heard Elizabeth Jayne Webb born and was able to talk briefly with Regina about our baby girl. The general consensus was that I had food poisoning, probably from some bad chicken. Regardless, it was a crazy twenty-four hours, but I will always be grateful for my friend handing me the phone and letting me hear the amazing birth of my daughter.

My daughter, Elizabeth Jayne Webb. Picture taken in Texas before we moved to Atlanta.

And so life moved on. Lewisville Hospital was sold to a major healthcare company, and my role changed again. By this time, I had completed graduate school and now had my master's degree in health administration. I was interviewing with the hospital chain for an assistant administration position when my next life changer walked in the door. Barry O'Brien provided me with an opportunity that would forever alter the direction of my life and send me on a path toward entrepreneurship and wealth, failure and success, and adventure, loss, and redemption.

Barry worked for a company called Link Scientific Imaging, which was a start-up that provided mobile MRI services to hospitals around the country. At the time, the company had only three mobile routes: one in Connecticut, one in Florida, and one in Texas. Barry was the CEO, and he approached me about overseeing operations and sales for the Texas and Florida markets. I initially told him no because I was going to be a hospital administrator, but Barry persisted. He flew me to Connecticut and interviewed me in his Datsun 240Z doing about 100 mph down the freeway. I soon met other team members, like Tom Crucitti and Brian Stone, and before I knew it, I had accepted the position.

MRI, or magnetic resonance imaging, technology had been developed in the early 1980s, but like the computer, it took a while for it to become common. MRI scanners were big and bulky and, frankly, too expensive for a lot of hospitals to own and operate. The kinds of imaging that MRIs are capable of producing were game changing, but as the computer proved, wholesale change can be hard to come by. Link Scientific was one of several companies that were capitalizing on the small to midsize hospitals interested in using the technology before investing in it. Barry hired me as the assistant vice president of operations, which meant that I was in charge of organizing the complicated logistics of mobile MRI services.

Today, it is easy to imagine a room in a hospital basement or in an imaging center with the big, doughnut-shaped scanner mounted dead center, but back then our scanners were mounted in mobile units that looked more like semitruck trailers than anything you'd find today. We'd operate them on a schedule, setting up shop on a cement pad in the parking lot of a hospital on Monday, running scans all day on patients, and then packing things up to move to another hospital Tuesday, and so on and so on. We'd hit some hospitals once a month and others once a week. It was a complicated dance of supply and demand. The more scans we did, the more the hospital understood the power of MRI and the easier it was for the sales team to sell. Because the industry was relatively new, we were constantly learning. Insurance reimbursements, Medicare, shipping, setting up and tearing down. It was baptism by fire in the complicated machinations of the American healthcare system and in operating a business.

I had learned a lot about the technical side of imaging in school and in my early jobs. I'd learned about the administrative side working at the hospital, but Barry O'Brien had given me a chance to learn about the business side of healthcare. He was also a great leader and motivator who did not cut corners with his employees. I remember him telling me to rent a midsize car, not a compact, and to stay in a Marriott, not a Motel 6. He cared. I learned quickly and in no time got to thinking that I was pretty hot shit. I was traveling back and forth to the central office in Connecticut, doing a pretty good job delivering in Texas, Florida, and now also in California and Kansas, and making a name for myself in the world of MRI. I knew it, too, and that only made the struggles at home harder. But I was riding high and thought that, in no time, I'd be making more money than I could have ever imagined or thought possible.

Speaking of home, I think from the outside, things probably looked pretty great—and in several respects, and for periods, they were. I liked my job and being part of the leadership team of the company. I loved my little daughter and watching her grow up. But

Regina and I were starting to have problems, and a lot of them had to do with me. I won't write about the details and I won't belabor the point, but I wish I'd been more understanding and a better husband. I put most of the blame on me. About two and a half years into my job at Link, Regina and I separated, went to counseling, and, after six months, decided to give it one more try. During this same time, I had a big falling out with my boss, Barry, to the point that we had to be separated at the corporate office one time to avoid a physical altercation. Barry was a mentor, and I hated the feeling of losing him. We repaired the damage later but that is another chapter. Back to Regina. Three days after I moved back home, our world changed again.

I've already written about the value of decisiveness and being willing to dive into something new when you don't feel ready, but I have found that the most important lessons in life are the ones you don't see coming. They are the ones that knock on your door in the middle of the night or blindside you on a Thursday afternoon. People you never expected to meet. Opportunities you hadn't considered or an afternoon phone call when you think you have everything going for you and you're on top of the mountain.

"Mr. Webb," the voice on the other end of the phone said when I answered in my office. "The company has been sold, and the chair you are sitting in needs to be vacated by the end of the day. You have no equity, so therefore you are terminated."

I was floored. I'd been running myself ragged trying to keep up with the job, my ego, and the fantasy that I was in control. It was like a bucket of cold water in the face, followed by a hard slap—and I suddenly saw the mistakes I had made following someone else's dream. But I also saw the opportunity I had uncovered. I went home that night uncertain of what to say to Regina. I got up the next morning and played a round of golf, which is when I realized that I should have been depressed and miserable, but I felt something different entirely. I felt resolve. By Monday, I was interviewing in Atlanta for a job in my newfound industry of MRI.

I'd spent almost ten years in Texas. I'd had three jobs, attended two universities, and made connections and a small name for myself in the industry. I learned the value of decisiveness and a different way to manage. I learned to trust my ability to dive into murky waters and emerge unharmed. I'd fallen victim to my own ego, and it had hurt me professionally and privately. But in my last twenty-four hours in the Lone Star State, I realized the most important lesson in life and the one that inspired the title of this book: Resilience is the most important thing in life and in business.

> **RESILIENCE IS THE MOST IMPORTANT THING IN LIFE AND IN BUSINESS. IT IS THE KEY INGREDIENT OF SUCCESS AND THE THING THAT WILL NEVER LET YOU DOWN.**

It is the key ingredient of success and the thing that will never let you down. I could have quit. I could have soothed self-pity in the bottom of a bottle, but instead, something wouldn't let me fall prey to the victimhood I'd seen so many times in my life. I took a shower, played a round of golf, and did what I had done my entire life—got back to work.

REDNECK RECAP

When opportunity presents itself, take the risk. Never give in to self-pity.

CHAPTER FOUR

SEEING THE FUTURE AND LEAVING THE PAST

Resilience: Over time, you learn when to step away, to find another path. Rather than beat your head against a stone wall, find a way around, over, or under that wall, and continue on the path of your choosing.

They offered me the job on the spot. I'd been fired in Dallas four days earlier and just one day after moving back in with Regina to make things work. After the interview and the job offer, I flew home to discuss things with Regina to ensure that we were on the same page in moving to Atlanta. She's a southerner, like me, so moving to Atlanta was not something either of us opposed, but we did have to navigate the sale of the house and the move. We decided that I'd go first, and she and Lizzie would stay behind for a little while, help manage the house situation, and then join me in six months.

logic, and relationships. I liked him a great deal, but I hated the way Tom treated him, and I hated the idea of an intelligent man like Will cowering under a CEO with a fragile ego and a vengeful heart.

For some reason, despite all his bluster and meanness, Tom seemed to liked me. I didn't have stock options, and I spent most of my time traveling, so he couldn't lord a whole lot over me. Plus, I was never intimidated by him. Maybe it was because I knew I was smart, maybe it was because I knew this job was a stepping-stone to some unknown future, or maybe I had just developed the kind of tough shell that comes from a struggling marriage, a sudden firing, and a life spent clawing and scratching for the things I wanted, but he didn't scare me. I could look him in the eye and know he was a tyrant, and I took a certain amount of comfort in that.

Six months after I arrived in Atlanta, Regina and Lizzie made the move to join me. I don't want to belabor our relationship's demise too much, nor do I want to flog myself excessively, but I certainly was not very good to my wife. Looking back, it's clear to me that we were over long before she came to Atlanta, and once she was there, I behaved in ways I still regret. I didn't cheat and I wasn't abusive, but I wasn't good to her either. Regina and I met in a world I aspired to leave behind, and over time it became clear that she never wanted the life I had led her on. While I was trying to change my future, Regina's aspirations were different. She never really wanted to leave Mississippi, and when the time came, I realized that she wasn't the partner I needed and that I wasn't the husband she deserved.

You learn a lot about yourself through the relationships you develop, and I guess that was the best part about Atlanta for me. Positive relationships teach in subtle ways. Negative ones are more explicit. I learned from Regina that I could never go back home. I could never settle back into that town, that way of life. I don't judge people for their desires, but I do wonder, when I see people choose ease over opportunity, why they do that.

Working for Will, I learned how nice people can be abused by tyrants. Tom was lucky to have Will. I was lucky to have met Will, and he helped me to learn the imaging center model. Working for him, I met people who would create opportunities for me moving forward, including Lynn.

Lynn is her real name, and I use it here because we are friends to this day. She was another regional manager, so our paths crossed quite a bit. Like me, she was learning about the burgeoning industry, and we often passed opportunities on to one another.

I stayed in Atlanta for only one year after Regina and Lizzie joined me. In all honesty, I'm not sure I would have stayed even if things hadn't happened the way I'm about to recount. I didn't love the city. I didn't love the company, and I had gotten to a point in my career where I wanted to climb up the ladder and accelerate at a pace of my own choosing. Everything was about to change for me, and I would learn quickly that things blowing up and things burning down can look an awful lot alike and can happen at the same time.

For this little piece of wisdom, I have only one person to thank, a Democratic congressman from California named Pete Stark.

MRI centers were part of a systemic, entrepreneurial change that was happening across healthcare in the 1990s. Private physician joint ventures were popping up like weeds after a rainstorm, offering services ordinarily

I WOULD LEARN QUICKLY THAT THINGS BLOWING UP AND THINGS BURNING DOWN CAN LOOK AN AWFUL LOT ALIKE AND CAN HAPPEN AT THE SAME TIME.

carried out at hospitals, ranging from blood work to MRI scans. In short, physicians now owned the facilities where they referred their own patients and, as such, billed insurance and made outside profits.

Pete Stark saw a problem with this. In 1988, he introduced the Ethics in Patient Referrals Act. If you need some reading to put you to sleep, I recommend you check it out, but the long and the short of it is that he, and others, didn't like the idea of doctors writing prescriptions for procedures that could be carried out by private clinics in which the doctors had a financial stake. Basically, he didn't want doctors to own both supply, in the form centers like those providing MRI, and demand, in the form of their prescription pads, and then expect insurance companies and Medicare to pick up the tab. He believed that a situation like this would create an ethical problem for doctors, who would be financially incentivized to order unnecessary procedures that would line their pockets and bilk the taxpayers. It's called self-referral.

I never really had a problem with these types of deals, if structured right. Give them a small ownership piece, don't pay them on what they send but pay them if the business is profitable based on their ownership percentage. By doing it this way, the doctor is incentivized to use the facility but not incentivized to abuse patients. I always compared it to owning Walmart stock. If I own Walmart stock, I'm going to shop at Walmart, but I'm not going to buy things I don't need or overshop. But healthcare creates strange dilemmas in perception, and we constantly had to navigate these waters.

The company I worked for was publicly traded, so there was no problem there, but Lynn had a friend, named Steve, who needed some help. Steve was a doctor in Florida who had made a nice pile of money for himself by pulling groups of doctors together to own imaging centers. There were fifteen in total, including three in Chicago (a fact that will become important later).

Lynn called to see if I'd be interested in going to work with Dr. Steve to straighten out the operations of his clinics. The Stark law was going into effect starting in 1994, and the state of Florida enacted a reciprocal law, which meant that all the ownership structure for his little empire had to be rethought, redesigned, and reestablished fairly quickly. Doctors needed to be bought out, corporate structures needed to be rewritten, and, in general, his medical imaging empire needed a whole lot of untangling. Lynn set up a meeting, and I soon found myself riding in a stretch limo from the Fort Lauderdale airport to a tree-shaded strip mall in Boca Raton.

Dr. Steve was pretty flashy, although the office was anything but, and yet I couldn't help but be tempted. There was a lot of potential in the opportunity he laid out, but there were two things I knew for certain: (1) I wanted out of the company I was working for, and (2) I needed an excuse to leave Regina. I know the latter sounds harsh, but the short time we had spent in Atlanta had really shown me that our paths were destined to diverge. I'm the kind of person who makes decisions quickly and that, sadly, was one of them.

I went back to Atlanta knowing what I wanted and turned in my two-week resignation to Will. Word must have traveled because a few days later, I was summoned to a meeting with Tom and the corporate lawyer.

We met in a conference room, the two of them on one side of the table and me on the other. Tom, who fancied himself a direct kind of person, which was code for asshole most of the time, cut right to the chase.

"James, I think you're smart and can do a lot of good here. I'm going to fire your boss [Will] and give you his job." He made a show of reaching for his wrist, taking off his Rolex, and putting it on the table. "I'll give you thirty seconds to decide."

It was like I was back in Mississippi flipping a coin, back on campus getting Regina's schedule to ask her out, back in every moment of my life when clarity created dead certainty. I spoke without hesitation or remorse.

"Tom, I don't need thirty seconds to decide. You can go fuck yourself."

I stood up and walked out of the room. His lawyer, a man I liked, chased me down the hall and stopped to tell me that this "exit" was one of the most amazing things he had ever seen and that no one had ever done that to Tom. He wasn't wrong. Quitting that job the way I did was one of my proudest moments. Tom thought he could bully me, but he couldn't, and it had been high time somebody told him what he could do. When I look back on that moment, it still brings a smile to my face. The company was eventually taken back private and Tom cashed out, leaving most of the folks hanging with worthless options. Like I said, he was a dick.

I have the opposite feeling when I think about what came next—telling Regina that I was moving to Florida without her. I tried hard to do the right thing, even if pride and history made it feel wrong. I knew moving on without her was the right thing for me to do, but that doesn't mean it didn't hurt her and Lizzie. And it doesn't mean it didn't hurt me. I truly regret having to do it, and I still think about it to this day. My beautiful daughter forgave me. Regina never did.

I accepted the job as chief operating officer working for Dr. Steve Schulman on July 1, 1992. By Christmas, my life would be changed forever.

REDNECK RECAP

When chasing opportunity, never compromise your principles. Sometimes you have to make tough personal decisions, and sometimes you have to walk away from bullies.

CHAPTER FIVE

EMBRACING CHANCE—
IN LIFE AND IN LOVE

Resilience: Confidence in your decisions can lead to
huge success or abject failure. But know when to take
the risk, and know you will recover if you fail.

I like to think that my life has had seasons, different segments representing very different experiences, priorities, and perspectives.

There were the early days (James 1.0), growing up in Laurel, Mississippi, working and finding my way to college, medical imaging, and Regina. They were the young years, making the kinds of mistakes that people that age do and, I guess, learning that I needed to grow up.

Then came the second part (James 2.0), which was about setting forth and figuring out life beyond Laurel. It was about identifying what I was good at, what I'd underestimated and misunderstood. I put my head down for much of this period of time and bulldozed my way forward, learning lessons but also leaving a path behind me—broken things, mistakes, and highs and lows.

Leaving Atlanta and Regina began the third chapter (James 3.0). Aside from the guilt that I felt leaving my daughter with her mom, what came next was an adventure, a crazy journey that I look back on and still have a hard time believing was ever a reality. There were risks and rewards, ideas and connections, love and terror, success and failure. There were moments when I thought the world was my oyster and others when, as I was staring down the end of a gun barrel, I wondered what kind of idiot I had been to get into such a mess.

But that comes later.

First, I had to leave behind the life I had known to step into one I didn't understand. My position as COO of Dr. Schulman's little empire meant that I technically reported to him, but he was off and running his business, so I was pretty much left to my own devices. I had a lot to figure out and knew from the moment I arrived in Boca Raton that I'd probably have to do most of it on my own.

I cannot underscore how important the Stark legislation was to changing the course of my life. Steve Schulman had built a lucrative business for himself and his partners, all of whom were physicians. But the Stark law meant that business had to be redesigned from the ground up and the inside out. New corporations had to be formed with new partners. Doctors had to be bought out and moved around, and we were doing it under great duress. States, the legislatures of which had to adopt the new measures since those bodies controlled how much federal healthcare dollars were spent, were adopting the same laws. They did so slowly at first, but they steadily gained steam. Florida, which has always been a little bit lawless, was where the majority of the company's imaging centers were, and the state legislature had essentially duplicated the Stark law. No physician ownership in virtually anything—and specifically medical imaging.

There were three centers in Illinois, including one that was under construction, and that state's lawmakers were just as quick to tackle Stark. I could see right away that we needed a plan of attack. There was a lot of work to do, but not every state or center was under the same pressure. We needed to triage, just like my days back in the ER in Mississippi, and take on the most urgent challenges first.

Complicating things immensely was the small fact that I was in the midst of a divorce from a woman who wasn't super eager to make things easy. I couldn't blame her, of course, but it meant that I was distracted and trying to find a bit of balance. I lived in and out of hotels, traveling around Florida, to Illinois, Virginia, Puerto Rico, and back to Georgia to see Lizzie. On top of it all, I was trying to manage my new boss's expectations.

After a few months, I eventually got an apartment in Boca Raton, which stands out clearly in my mind because it was the first time I had lived on my own. I'd lived at home when I was at Jones County Junior College, and by the time I went off to finish my undergraduate degree, Regina and I had been married. While we were apart, I'd lived in corporate accommodations, but home had always been with her. It was a strange experience to be standing in my own apartment for the first time in my life in my early thirties. Regina and Lizzie had moved back to Mississippi, where Regina still lives today. As I've said, I don't blame people for wanting things to stay the same, but if your aspirations aren't in the same ballpark as your partner's, it's a no-win situation.

Work was a blur of meetings—with lawyers, staff, owners, and doctors. I didn't have to do much of the heavy lifting when it came to the corporate structural changes. My attention was focused on operations, to make sure the centers were running, and on marketing, to make sure they were viable.

Chicago seemed to need the most work, so once my personal life got a bit more settled, I spent a lot of time there. There were two imaging centers up and running in Chicago. The third, a new operation in the River North neighborhood, was under construction, a project that I was involved in and that was run by a contractor named Budd Fischer.

Budd was Steve Schulman's first cousin, and he and I hit it off right away. He remains my best friend to this day, but our relationship is a lot more complicated than that. This is, in no small part, because not long after he and I began working together, I fell in love with his daughter, a woman who would change my life more times than I can count.

Marcia Beth Fischer was in sales for the company in the Chicago market, and she was a killer. Smart, confident, beautiful. I think I knew the moment we met that there was something special about her.

I was in my office in Chicago, sitting at my desk and doing some work. I was still new to the company, and I made myself available to anyone who wanted to get to know me—a meet-the-new-boss kind of thing. There were some people I enjoyed meeting, and there were others who I knew were probably not long for employment. But when Marcia walked in, I knew it was something different. I remember to this day her velvet dress and the shine on her black patent leather shoes. I didn't know she was Budd's daughter. I didn't even know her name, but I can say without a hint of hesitation that I wanted to know more about her.

Our relationship began professionally. Marcia was in charge of imaging center sales for the Chicago market, and my responsibilities included establishing new marketing practices to make sure the centers would thrive after doctors were no longer involved as owners. It was natural that we spent a lot of time together. I knew in the back of my mind what I wanted, but I also knew from experience—both mine and others'—that dating in the workplace can be absolute poison to an office culture, particularly between someone in a position of authority and a person who reports to them.

This was 1992. Bill Clinton had not been outed for his relationship with Monica Lewinsky, but we were fresh on the heels of Clarence Thomas and Anita Hill. Sexual politics in the workplace had taken on a new cultural momentum and what had once been something whispered about over the water fountain was now front-page news. Our company had experienced this when we had to fire someone in one of our centers for an inappropriate relationship. There had even been a lawsuit related to workplace relationships gone bad that, as COO, eventually crossed my desk, but I couldn't help thinking about Marcia.

One of my favorite early photos of Marcia.

There are those who think Marcia was the reason I decided to end my first marriage, but divorce proceedings were in the works before the two of us had even met. I tried to keep things platonic between us, but that didn't last very long. One of the blessings of my innate decisiveness is that I am able to move forward while others waiver. I can spot and take advantage of opportunities while others are still thinking about things. There are disadvantages as well, and chief among them is that once I decide something, I don't have the patience to wait … I just go get it.

Apparently the feeling was mutual, and we began quietly dating a couple of months later, knowing that we were playing with fire. She worked for me. Her dad was a contractor for the company. Her dad's cousin was my boss, and our company was in the midst of a lawsuit for a situation not all that different from the one we were creating for ourselves.

In business, you develop a relationship with risk. For some people, they avoid risk at all costs. They may not make it big, but they don't lose a lot either. Other people are cavalier. They take huge swings and strike out a bunch in pursuit of that one perfect home run. Still others, people like me, approach risk from a different angle. We don't regret the big risks we didn't take. That's a fool's errand. I can't tell you how many times I've heard some blowhard talk about how they "almost" did something. Almost gets you nothing. You either did something or you didn't. You either stepped up to the plate or you watched from the stands, but you were never almost in the game.

I look at risk as a calculation. If a risk is huge and comes with a big upside, I'm suspicious but interested, and I'll follow that interest until the risk-to-reward relationship either becomes untenable or irresistible. I'm no adrenaline junkie, but I'm not afraid to take a shot either. With everything that was going on, dating Marcia was a risk, but it was a calculated one. I knew that I was moving into a new phase in my life, and she was the kind of person I wanted to share that phase with.

In many ways, she was the partner I wanted, but in many more, she was the partner I needed. She was strong and confident, unapologetic and smart, but caring and generous as well. She came from a family completely unlike my own. Illinois bred, Jewish, and big city. I would come to admire and love them as my own and still do to this day.

But that would come later. For now, I had a short-term, secret relationship with a woman I should not have had anything to do with only a few months into accepting a new job after telling my old boss, quite literally, to go fuck himself.

It was clear from the beginning that there was a lot of potential—reward—with our relationship. It wasn't a casual thing, but I would never know just how far things might go as long as we kept "us" a secret. I had to know if the risk would pay off, and the best opportunity to know came at Thanksgiving in 1992. The company was having a management dinner after a day at the radiology show. Steve Schulman was there. The corporate attorney was there. And Budd Fischer was there, among others. I was invited, of course, and it was suggested that I could bring a date. OK, time for my move. Marcia and I went for a drink before dinner and arrived after most of the people were already seated.

THERE'S NO SUCH THING AS A SAFE INVESTMENT. EVERYTHING YOU DO COMES WITH RISK.

We hadn't talked about it, but we both knew it was the right moment. Walking into that room holding Marcia's hand was like stepping off a cliff. In the calculation between risk and reward, there is seldom certainty. You don't know when you leave for work that you will come home that night. There's no such thing as a safe investment. Everything you do comes with risk. You hardly think about the things for which the risk is extremely low—brushing your teeth or sweeping the floor. And you can talk yourself out of the things where the risk is high—skydiving or swimming with sharks. The little voice in your head that discourages you from doing those things is the part of you that calculates that the reward probably isn't worth it—a couple of moments of free fall versus ending up as roadkill, touching a shark versus losing an arm. If that voice is strong enough, you walk away. I'm pretty good at knowing when to listen to that voice, but on that night in November 1992, the little voice wasn't telling me to run. It was telling me to grasp her hand and take a chance.

The reward of walking into that room together was enormous; the reward for walking away didn't exist. In this case, the biggest risk would have been to do nothing.

It was the best chance I have ever taken.

I sat down next to Steve, chugged a glass of Greek wine, and then leaned into him and whispered, "Do I still have a job?"

Steve paused, smiled, and said, "I couldn't be happier." A short time later, I talked to Budd as well, and he told me to behave myself and that he was OK with it. The only person that night who turned three shades of sickly green was the corporate attorney—who was still fighting the lawsuit related to a workplace relationship gone bad—until we looked at each other, shook our heads, and laughed. Over time, Budd and the Fischer family welcomed me into their lives.

Our relationship survived on weekend visits and evening phone calls, vacations and holidays, from 1992 to 1995, when Marcia finally moved to Florida. Was it perfect? Whatever is? But I knew that, in her, I had found the partner I needed in my life. I knew it in the moment, and looking back, it is even clearer, because just as our relationship was an adventure and represented a new beginning in my personal life, the job that made it possible also sent me on a journey that would leave me forever changed.

REDNECK RECAP

Business and personal relationship are there for the taking. Be decisive and never run from the risk.

CHAPTER SIX

NO ROOM FOR A BULLDOZER

Resilience: Know your strengths and hire others as strong, if not stronger, to ensure that your shortfalls are covered. Never give up on love. And when opportunity knocks, jump.

I did a lot of listening in my first six months at International Magnetic Imaging (IMI). The company had to change. The new self-referral laws were the driving force behind this required change, and Steve Schulman and his partners needed someone to come in and set things straight. I was looking, they were looking, and we found each other through a mutual contact. Before Steve and I met, we had been on opposites sides of the proposed Stark legislation. I worked for a company that supported the removal of physician ownership, and Steve was the poster child for doctors investing in imaging centers. For all practical purposes, I was the right guy for the job.

After I accepted the position at IMI in July 1992, and for about six months before moving to Florida, I lived my life out of hotels and suitcases. I spent time in all the markets—Florida, Illinois, Virginia, and Puerto Rico—talking to the staff and listening to what they had to say and then figuring out the clearest path forward. It was obvious that although every market and every imaging center had its own challenges, the thing that was missing was on-the-ground clinic leadership, and I was fortunate that the partners gave me a lot of room to provide it.

I'm not the kind of person to sit down and read management books. You'll find Peter Drucker on my bookshelf, but I don't spend a lot of time learning new approaches. However, Kenneth Blanchard and Spencer Johnson's *The One-Minute Manager* is the exception. If you haven't read the book, it's probably the clearest summary of my preferred management approach. Contingency management is a philosophy built on the idea that there is no unilateral management style that works for everyone. Some people need a cheerleader, others need a hard-ass. As a believer in the contingency approach, it was my job to understand the people of IMI: what did they see, what did they think, what did they need, what did they want, and who needed to go and who needed to stay.

A lot of people needed to go in those first few months I was with the company, and I spent a lot of time and energy making that happen. It wasn't a hatchet job. I didn't come in with the expectation that I needed to clean house, but it was the right thing to do. As often happens in companies, quite a few people had climbed the ranks based on nothing more than duration and a demonstrated competency for one job that was mistranslated into a promotion into another. People who had been with IMI from day one had been put into management roles where they didn't belong. It was the Peter principle, pure and simple. People rose to the level of their incompetency.

It's never easy letting someone go, as I have done numerous times throughout my career. I take no pleasure in the act of firing or terminating someone, but a big part of my role was to right the company ship. The corporate attorney and partners were busy restructuring IMI to prepare for Stark, and I had to get the company prepared for what would follow—competition. Prior to Stark, doctors might own a small piece of an imaging center. They had a built-in loyalty to send patients to those clinics. I still don't believe it was a big enough reason to do anything unethical. In fact, the Stark law made it worse. Because a physician could no longer be part of a joint venture, they started buying their own machines. This found the doctor in debt, with a machine and staff to pay for, so they began to write all the orders they wanted to pay off their investment and make a few bucks. On the other side of the spectrum, once doctors no longer had a vested interest in sending patients to one clinic or another, competition would be coming fast and furious. If we didn't have the right people in the right roles with the right goals and the right incentives, we would be eaten alive by new conglomerates and mom-and-pop shops. Change wasn't just timely; it was vital.

Over the course of my career, I've probably terminated 250 people, and I'm proud to say that I still receive Christmas cards from around 248 of them. You're probably thinking that I'm full of it, but I'm not. It's never easy to fire someone, but that doesn't mean you have to be a jerk about it. As a manager, if the person you are letting go is surprised by it, you have failed in your duty to that person. I place a big premium on creating clarity for those

MANAGEMENT IS A SERVICE, NOT A POWER PLAY.

people I manage and, per the contingency approach, adjust how that clarity comes to life based on their needs, not mine. Management is a service, not a power play. Your job is to provide people with the best possible chance to succeed in their job by ensuring that they are in the right job, making the objectives of that job crystal clear, supporting their

centage) pipeline was going away. We couldn't rely on referrals from vested partners. We needed to rethink the customer pipeline, which meant understanding our customers a lot better than we ever had. MRI technology was reaching ubiquity in American medicine, and it would be difficult to create any point of market differentiation based on our scans. Instead, it seemed to me that there were a few crucial relationships we needed to think about: the relationship between our radiologists and our doctors, the relationship between our sales function and our doctors' offices, and the relationship between patients and the experience we create for them. And if we wanted to protect our business, we needed to get to work quickly.

Doctors' offices are a little like kingdoms. At the top is the doctor, the monarch, but anybody who has ever read a fairy tale or studied history knows that one head may wear the crown, but the real power stands at either side of the throne.

IMI had marketing programs in place, but it looked like they catered more to investors than to customers. Go to a nice lunch, give the doctor their distribution, and you were probably in pretty good shape. But now we needed to think of the whole chain of command. Without the potential for backend profit, doctors cared very little about where the scans they ordered were done. In fact, they cared more about where *not* to do the scans, mostly due to bad experiences for them and their patients. The office managers were the centers of power in the doctors' offices, followed by the nurses, the RNs, and the scheduling manager. Each of them looked for different things. The office manager needed to be respected and heard. The nurses and RNs needed results and to know that the people they sent in for a scan were being taken care of. The scheduling manager needed a good relationship, a positive experience, and people who were easy to work with.

Marketing and operations, in other words, were inextricably linked.

We created programs around those three key relationships and set expectations for our people to make those relationships as strong as possible.

When I was young and coming up in the imaging world, radiologists and techs were like phantoms—seldom seen, lurking in the background, carrying out their work alone in quiet rooms away from the fray. We needed our radiologists to be more than experts in technology. We needed them to be partners to doctors and nurses in the care of their patients. That meant that they had to be quick, to turn around test results faster than might be expected with maximum accuracy, and to make themselves available to medical staff for consultation. For some of our folks, it made sense. For others, though, the new expectations of overdelivering didn't sit right. Some of them left and a few even tried to open their own centers, with varying degrees of success.

Our sales staff could no longer rely on just dropping off stuff for the office staff to keep them happy. We trained and expected them to listen, to observe, and to change their thinking from selling scans to serving needs. Just as we had experienced with radiologists, this rubbed some folks the wrong way. Two particular managers in the Chicago offices didn't seem to like the new way of thinking.

I realize that I come with a lifetime of biases to this story, but I think I saw Marcia's potential two minutes after I met her. She was hard charging, smart, and ambitious. She represented the new way we needed to operate before it had been articulated. And the two managers in Chicago clearly had a problem with her style. Just as quickly as I had recognized Marcia's talent, I recognized that these two people were, like some in South Florida, the walking embodiment of the Peter principle.

Although the partners, lawyers, and senior management knew that Marcia and I were dating, these two managers in Chicago did not. Every time I'd arrive at their clinics, they would start bitching and fussing about Marcia and her methods, even calling her explicit names. I kept my cool and tried to work with both to get them to embrace this needed change. And then the holiday party happened. I will never forget the look on the two managers' faces when Marcia and I walked into the room holding hands. I honestly think they peed themselves. The next week, I met with both managers individually. One was pretty cool with it and said, "I probably don't have a job now, do I?" I said probably not, and we laughed about it as he noted that he had learned a lesson. The other manager didn't take it well and then sued me and the company with an outright lie claiming that I had told her to "blow doctors" to get referrals. I never said that, and she was caught in her lie at her new job—bragging about it and the lawsuit to a new fellow employee whose sister just happened to work for us. Our attorneys depositioned the "witness" and got the former manager fired from her new job and had the lawsuit dismissed.

While the lawyers and owners worked out the challenges of reorganization, I focused on getting the right people into the right roles, minimizing the Peter principle's effect and focusing on making IMI a well-oiled machine. It was becoming a really fun job and was exactly what I needed.

The difficult things at IMI were remedied over the course of the first year, and by my second year in the job, I had settled into a groove. Eventually, I started developing a bit of a bigger name for myself in the world of medical imaging. I cultivated relationships with doctors and radiologists, office managers, vendors, and manufacturers, but the one that would prove the most important for everything that came after my time at IMI was the one I built with the man who had brought me into the fold in the first place.

Steve Schulman was a lot of things. He was a doctor, an entrepreneur, and a mentor of sorts. He never lacked vision, and he helped me to form a perspective that changed my life, a single thought that comes to mind every time I hear politicians and pundits debate what has become one of the lightning-rod issues of twenty-first-century America: healthcare.

It all boils down to a simple thought that I'll say here because I have no shame in thinking it—there is absolutely nothing wrong with making money in healthcare, provided making money does not come at the detriment of the patient. I learned that from Steve, who knew better than most that capitalism drives innovation through competition. Every time I listen to some doe-eyed politician try to score points by railing against the big, bad "corporations" that are hell-bent on robbing and killing the very patients who need them, I have to roll my eyes. To these people, healthcare is a human right—something I don't disagree with. Everyone has the right to be healthy, but I subscribe to the belief that the best way to be healthy is to incentivize healthcare providers to overdeliver in order to stay in business.

I grew up working in hospitals and know the smug self-righteousness that comes from believing that you are somehow noble for eschewing private practice to stay close to patients. But let me tell you something: There is no place where the patient matters less than in a large community hospital—where the staff gets paid regardless of the outcome and competition doesn't exist. You'll understand what I mean more clearly a couple of chapters farther along, but suffice it to say that when people rail against healthcare capitalism, they demonstrably understand very little about both healthcare and improving the quality of patient care.

Steve and his partners built IMI in a white space—private imaging centers were relatively new, even newer than the technology they relied on—but as the industry grew and matured, as the Stark law changed the landscape, it became clear that the only way to survive and continue to grow was to provide what couldn't be received in hospitals—superior service that focused on the patient's needs, their providers' needs, and the community's needs.

That's where capitalism comes into play. Ask any capitalist what matters the most and they won't tell you that innovation or one-of-a-kind opportunities are the things that keep them in business. It's the ability to really understand a customer's needs, move quickly to deliver on those needs, and do it all for a reasonable price that keeps them in the black but below the competition.

A lot of people don't want to talk about healthcare in a capitalistic context. Let's look at another thing people don't want, but require, in a world without competition: driver's licenses.

Like healthcare, having a driver's license is a requirement for participating and thriving in a modern world. Even if you don't drive, good luck getting on a plane, registering to vote, or applying for a bank account without that tiny piece of plastic, whether a driver's license or a government-issued ID. There's only one place to get a driver's license—the Department of Motor Vehicles, a place so famous for awful service, long lines, random price changes, rude people, and needless hassle that it has become a universal punch line in American life. There's no incentive for the DMV to provide more comfortable chairs, reduce wait times, improve efficiency, focus on customer service, or help you out. The people who work there don't make the rules, and they get paid whether you get what you need or not. They are going home when the "closed" sign is turned, regardless of what you need.

Now imagine a world where private companies could get involved in providing IDs. Not in the for-profit prison way, where competition is artificially limited by legislation, but in an open marketplace. What do you think would happen? Getting a driver's license would no longer be the joke that it is. Don't believe me? When was the last time you went to the post office? And why has the cost of shipping not increased over the last twenty years, despite a growth in volume? FedEx, UPS, DHL—all the shipping companies is why. They got into the market and forced the USPS to compete in order to survive.

Don't get me wrong. I know that capitalism can create some world-class creeps and evil companies doing evil things, but if your first priority is creating the best outcome for patients and you are incentivized to deliver those outcomes, then you shouldn't have to apologize for making a profit.

That's why Steve Schulman remains on my list of the most influential people in my life. He helped me understand that patients are customers, and the customer is always king. But so are doctors, office managers, and staff. If you are genuine in your ethics and efforts to provide an unparalleled offering to the people who need it, and that becomes your focus, then you have no reason to hide it and no interest in listening to the talking heads argue over their plans.

On the personal side, Marcia and I traded weekends in Florida and Chicago, went on vacations, and spent as much time together as we could. I hadn't set out to find her—or anyone, for that matter—when I left Atlanta, but as I've said, its rarely the things you set out to do that have the biggest influence on your life. You can't plan to fall in love, and there have been a few times in my life, some of which I'll reveal in later chapters, when following my instincts, without any semblance of a plan in mind, has served me well. It wasn't just Marcia either but her family. Her father, Budd, and I grew to be very close friends, and her Mom and siblings and the rest of the family had accepted me, Baptist redneck from Mississippi, as one of their own.

Me and Marcia at our wedding, 1995.

Marcia eventually moved to Florida and we got married. I wasn't a wealthy man, but I was thriving and successful in the eyes of the corporate world. Steve and his partners seemed happy, and were making enough to keep them in limos and nice houses. We bought a little place in Boca Raton, with a pool and a small cabana house that I eventually used as an office, and about eighteen months after we got married, Marcia told me she was pregnant with our first son. I'd come a long way from Laurel and a long way from the world I'd left behind. On paper, everything looked pretty good—really good, in fact—and had it been someone else, I don't think I would have blamed them for riding that wave as far as it would take them. But I'm not most people.

I've never believed that happiness or success is the result of passion. In fact, I don't believe in solely following your passion. I believe in opportunity—in recognizing opportunity and seizing it. Working for IMI had been a great opportunity, but it was a job opportunity, someone else's opportunity for me, and I knew that I would never really be satisfied until I was in a position to create opportunities of my own. Steve had shown me how to think like a capital-

> **I BELIEVE IN OPPORTUNITY— IN RECOGNIZING OPPORTUNITY AND SEIZING IT.**

ist, feel like a caregiver, and create opportunities out of the overlap between my head and my heart if I were willing to take a chance.

That's why, one day in my fifth year with IMI, I realized what had to happen after I received a phone call from a doctor I knew. I was as certain as I had been about the need to get out of Laurel. As certain as I had been that I wouldn't work for a man in Atlanta who would count thirty seconds on his Rolex while I decided whether to take a new job. As certain that the woman with the patent leather shoes was unlike any other I had ever met.

Shortly after that call, I asked Steve if we could meet. I looked my friend and mentor in the eye, the man who had taught me so much and who had become much more like family than a boss, and I said, "I've got a crazy idea, and I need you to fire me."

REDNECK RECAP

Management is not a power play. It is a means to an end and requires that you find and lead the right people to the next finish line.

some, like George, who had exploited a loophole in the law that allowed private practitioners to be owners of the technology as long as it was on the doctor's office premises and part of the practice's corporate structure. George and others ponied up the money and bought their own CT scanner, but they soon realized that to make the financial recoup numbers work, it was impossible for their practices to serve enough patients who might need imaging services. Those CT scanners are expensive to buy and expensive to run, and most doctors couldn't see enough patients in a day to make it work.

As an example, imagine that you love ice cream. You love it so much that you decide you want to buy a piece of a local ice-cream shop—5 percent or so. But then a law is written that says you can't eat ice cream and own a portion of an ice-cream shop, but you can put an ice-cream shop in your living room. So you take out a loan, build the shop, and charge the people in your house to eat your ice cream. There is simply no way for you to make enough money from your spouse and kids eating ice cream to pay the loan on the shop, not to mention the supplies and maintenance. What do you do?

If you're George Laquis, you call a guy who owns ice-cream shops and ask him for help.

At first, George was hoping to find a way for IMI to operate his machine for him, but the economics and the laws wouldn't allow this idea to work. Eventually, he decided to sell us the scanner, and that process served as the basis of our friendship. I liked George a lot. He was fun to be around, worldly, and smart, and we were similar in our thinking. He was an idealist but pragmatic, and I always looked forward to the times we got together.

It was George who called me about eighteen months after that deal and inspired me to ask Steve Schulman to fire me. After years of practice in the US, he had decided that it was time to move back home and get serious about his dream to take care of his countrymen by becoming the minister of health. It wasn't a lock, of course. Politics are politics, whether you're in Washington, DC, or on an island in the Caribbean, and George knew that he couldn't just walk into the ministry and ask for the job. George also knew that Trinidad needed medical imaging services, which is when he called me.

Even as George laid out the idea, I knew it probably wasn't something that Steve, his partners, and IMI would or should be interested in. Buying a new machine and finding a way to get it to Trinidad, and then get it installed and set up a business in an unfamiliar market and government environment, was a lot of hassle with big risks and a murky upside. I knew that if I took the idea to Steve, he would say no. Hell, I would advise him to say no. But it was just the kind of opportunity I had been waiting for, even if I didn't know it.

The only problem was, I didn't have any money. That's why I needed Steve Schulman to fire me.

My plan was pretty simple, even if it wasn't completely thought through. I would ask Steve to fire me instead of me quitting, and I would receive a six-month severance payout. I would also ask him to be the first investor in my new company. In addition, I decided that I'd rely on George's connections and influence to get the whole thing up and running—and figure everything else out from there. Like I said, it wasn't completely thought out, but then again, none of my businesses and none of my best ideas ever have been. It's the ones that I plot out and overthink that tend to fail, and looking back, there's no way anyone could accuse me of having overthought this thing.

But I was determined. I had spent my entire life—since I started cutting grass at eight years old—working for other people, and I wanted to work for myself. I never wanted to punch a time clock again, and thank the Lord, I never have. I think Steve knew there was no way I would go back to being his employee if he declined. He knew me well enough to know that once I made up my mind, there was little he (or anyone) could do to change it.

"I know you don't want to do this," I told him. "But I do."

I put him in a tough position. He could say no to bankrolling an opportunity that I admitted was wrong for his company but that would mean losing me to either another company or to someone else who would be willing to take a gamble on a guy with no real entrepreneurial experience but with a fire in his belly. Or he could go along with my proposal, which would mean I'd no longer be running IMI, and he could take some of the money he made and bet it on me to turn it into more.

I'm sure the fact that I was married to his cousin played into his decision. Family, even extended family, was important. But I'd also like to think that he saw how serious I was and that I made a convincing enough case to sway him. Either way, Steve said yes to my proposal and Paradigm Healthcare was born.

> **I HAD A CALLING, ONE THAT AROSE FROM MY BELIEF IN OPPORTUNITY OVER PASSION AND AN INNATE TRUST IN MY GUT INSTINCT WHEN IT CAME TO LIFE-ALTERING DECISIONS.**

I named the company Paradigm because starting my own company represented a major shift in my life (James 4.0). I was my own boss. I owned a minority stake in the company, owed Steve more money than the sum of my worldly possessions, and was just naive enough to think it might be easy. For the first time in my adult life, I didn't have a job. I had a calling, one that arose from my belief in opportunity over passion and an innate trust in my gut instinct when it came to life-altering decisions. And I had six months of severance to prove it.

Steve helped me finance an MRI machine, and I powered through the logistics of shipping it from the US on a barge to Port of Spain, Trinidad. But before we could set up shop, we needed to get the blessing of the Trinidad government. George was willing to help set up meetings but couldn't be involved financially in the deal. It was our pitch—my pitch—to make. If it went well, George would get some credit that would help him in his aspiration to become the minister of health, but if it didn't, he needed to be able to distance himself, which I understood.

Because of his commitment to IMI, Steve preferred to be a silent partner; we needed a third member of our team to help with money and to lend additional credibility to our proposal. Joe Paul, an acquaintance who managed imaging centers in Florida, was willing to come along for the ride. He and I went to the Ministry of Health in Trinidad to plead our case. We needed the minister's permission to operate and made a compelling argument for the benefits that our technology would bring to his country. We walked in feeling optimistic. We walked out disappointed, with no clear answer or direction

I was probably a little dejected, but I don't tend to wallow. Resilience, after all, is what I attribute every success in my life to, so Joe and I, with some help from George, made a plan. The next week, we took out a full-page article in the island's daily paper to demonstrate to the ministry that we were serious. The article alluded to the miracle of the technology and the opportunities afforded to doctors in providing the best healthcare possible—the care their patients deserved. We even referenced that we were coming independent of government approval. It was a not-so-subtle message to the ministry, which miraculously changed course and approved our plan to build an MRI center and put it in an empty field next to the soccer stadium. Just like that we were in business. Shortly thereafter, Joe got a great offer to head up a new publicly traded imaging center company. He asked me if I wanted to join him, but I couldn't let go of this Trinidad opportunity. We parted as friends and now see each other about once a year at the radiology trade show.

I bought the magnet secondhand from a dealer who had done work with me before and shipped the twenty-four-thousand-pound medical miracle on a barge in a twenty-four-foot by forty-eight-foot mobile office to an island fourteen miles off the South American coast. We shipped people in, too, from Miami and Puerto Rico, to install the machine and get it up and running. Next, we needed to find people qualified to operate the machine and run the business.

In 1996, Trinidad was a world of contrasts. A lot of the island was built through British colonialism and, later, the oil and gas industry. It wasn't necessarily pretty, but there were parts that seemed other-worldly and incredible. There are no big cities, just towns and villages that seem to have come together more by accident than by design. It is the home of Carnival, an annual festival of parades, skimpy outfits, and Calypso music.

I used to walk through the Savannah when I wasn't working. A giant park in the middle of the capital city, it is full of vendors and markets and artisans. It's also the place where, one evening, I saw three men hanging from ropes on some gallows, an unsubtle warning to would-be criminals.

I offer all this as context to the incredible thing that happened when we began looking for a staff. Without connections and long before the days of LinkedIn, we put an ad in the local newspaper for a manager and struck gold. Chris Camacho was the first person to apply, and he just happened to have a master's degree in nuclear and MRI physics from the University of Toronto. He was a Trinidadian and had come home looking for a place to put his education to work.

We hired him on the spot. Our second employee, who we tasked with helping us market the operations of the center, was Luanne George. She was bright, personable, and connected and just happened to be a former runner-up to Miss Trinidad and Tobago.

Like I said, we struck gold.

We planned a ribbon-cutting ceremony and invited bigwigs from across the island. The local Catholic bishop showed up to bless the machine and nearly gave me a heart attack when he began throwing holy water on a giant, nuclear-powered electromagnet. But, thankfully, our biggest fears never came to pass.

I went back and forth between Florida and Trinidad monthly, staying in a Hilton hotel built into the side of a cliff and going from doctor to doctor to educate and market the technology. It reminded me a lot of the early days of MRI. Doctors were eager but wary. They needed to understand the use and benefits of the technology beyond just the surface-level information. But, unlike American doctors in those early years, Trinidadian doctors couldn't order a test and trust that the government's insurance plan or the patient's private insurance would cover the bills. Heck, we weren't even sure if any of the country's insurance plans would pay us. In addition, patients paid for a lot of healthcare out of their pockets on the island, and doctors were not only experts in medicine but also helped families manage their medical budgets.

As exciting as the technology was, doctors were understandably leery about handing the gringo two parties' hard-earned money, but that didn't prevent us from getting off the ground. It took a little extra work, but we were soon seeing eight patients a day and drawing them not only from the island but also from mainland South America. I wouldn't call it an overwhelming success, but we were in operation, and I was in control of my own destiny, which felt amazing.

Paradigm's Trinidad center was not even open when we were contacted by another South Florida doctor with a proposition. Allan Herskowitz was a Miami-based neurologist with connections to Nicaragua. He had an employee, a former doctor, who had fled the country to get away from the Sandinista National Liberation Front, a far-left militant organization that had ousted the dictatorial Somoza regime in the late 1970s and that was engaged in the ongoing Contra war with a whole lot of parties, including the CIA. This ex-doctor was still connected with the medical community in Managua and was ready to go home. After spending some time with Allan, I proposed that we try a joint venture with doctors there to install an imaging center that would serve the community. There was no Stark law in Nicaragua, and I was eager to try new things.

It didn't sound like a bad deal, and I was probably the perfect mix of naive, cocky, and thirsty for adventure to entertain the idea seriously. I was married to a woman who understood my need to build and grow, working out of the cabana next to our pool and ready to take on the world.

I put together a presentation and flew to Managua, where I was picked up at the airport and driven to the Intercontinental Hotel. Allan had helped arrange for me to have a driver and connected me with a lawyer who could assist with translation of everything from paperwork to dinner menus. I was given a tour of the city, which was poor and rundown. Poverty in the US looked cushy compared to what I saw there. I was taken to the palace, from which the Somoza regime had operated, and it was completely empty—a relic, a husk, a shell. It was eerie and exciting at the same time, reminding me of one of those temples in which Indiana Jones would find himself searching for treasure. I couldn't know it then, but the metaphor of a wide-eyed adventurer looking for treasure in a forgotten place would turn out to be apt for my time in Nicaragua.

We gathered a group of doctors together and fed them for the presentation. Our pitch was simple—a $2,000 investment earned a partnership in the venture. The more partners, the more referrals. The more referrals, the more money divided. There were a couple dozen of them, and although my pitch was slowed by translation, I thought I did a good enough job to get them ready to invest. I guess that's why I was a little surprised, and maybe hurt, that only one of them showed any interest in getting involved.

Looking back, I think it was pride and the intoxication of calling the shots that made me do what I did next. If given the same feedback today, I would probably just walk away. No, I would definitely walk away. But, like I said, I was naive and cocky enough to think I could make it all work out. I convinced my partners, Allan and Steve, that we should go it alone. We bought another machine and set it up in Managua, but unlike in Trinidad, where we were able to bring in a steady stream of patients with relative ease, things in Nicaragua didn't go smoothly.

MRI imaging center in Managua, Nicaragua.

Over the next two and a half years, I flew to Managua fifty-three times, trying to convince doctors to send patients our way, but they were slow to do so. There was virtually no health insurance, and almost all payments were made in cash. We were doing a couple of scans a day, but that was not enough. If I had known each time I went down there how little progress I would make, I would have simply bribed the doctors with a referral fee, but I didn't. It was the same problem we faced in Trinidad, where the doctors were wary to order scans that would take money out of their own pockets. But in Nicaragua, there was even less money to go around.

I was too bullheaded to see failure staring me in the face, and my sense of pride and overwhelming sunk-cost bias wouldn't let me quit. Marcia was working some and was the breadwinner. I wasn't making any money and was cobbling together consulting gigs during my time in Florida to keep a roof over our heads and food on the table. What money had been coming in from Trinidad was offset by loss in Nicaragua. We looked at deals in other countries—Honduras, Guatemala, Barbados, the Bahamas, and even Guyana, South America but things just weren't taking off the way I had hoped.

I WAS TOO BULLHEADED TO SEE FAILURE STARING ME IN THE FACE, AND MY SENSE OF PRIDE AND OVERWHELMING SUNK-COST BIAS WOULDN'T LET ME QUIT.

If I had gone into business in the US, I would have known what I was doing and not been blinded by the adventure of it all, and, man, what an adventure it was. Do I have any regrets? Of course I do, but in retrospect, it was part of the learning curve that ultimately brought me success.

I became good friends with my local lawyer and fixer in Managua. One night he took me to dinner far outside the city. We drove for what felt like an eternity into a thick jungle until we reached a clearing, parked, and set off on a trail that led to a restaurant nestled among the trees. We walked across a footbridge, and I looked at the water a few feet below. It was teeming with alligators, and on either side of the door, there were two jaguars chained to columns just far enough away to prevent any carnage. I don't know if I was scared or just awestruck, but in retrospect, it sure was a cool sight.

One morning in Managua, I got up and decided to go for a run. The Sandinistas were in power. They ran the military and the police, they had a stranglehold on the city, even if they didn't occupy higher offices, and they loved their guns. There were guns everywhere I looked, which should have told me not to wander far, but my run was going well, and I felt like exploring. I turned a corner and ran smack into a Contra street rally. The Contras were opposed to the Sandinistas. Hundreds, if not thousands, of people were chanting and cheering and firing their guns into the air. I felt like I was in one of those old western movies where the outlaw walks into the saloon and the music stops, people go silent, and all eyes fall on the stranger. I turned immediately and ran my ass off to get back to the hotel.

My biggest Indiana Jones moment came when I decided to take a day trip to an active volcano called Volcán Masaya. I made my way to the top and found a handmade, ladderlike device that stretched out over the mouth of the volcano. I can't remember exactly, but there was a little plaque that read "127 steps to Christ" or at least that's how I translated it. I've never been an adrenaline junky, but for some reason, I knew I had to climb out on that ladder and stare down into the lava, the pure pits of hell. It was rickety and swayed with each step. I was roughly two-thirds along when I noticed the Sandinista soldier at the other end staring at me from a couple of hundred yards away. He was all by himself, guarding an empty mountain. That was his job. I paused and watched him watching me. After a second or two, he raised his rifled and pointed it at me. I froze. Moments before, it had been an adventure. Now I was seriously wondering what the hell I was doing there. If he shot me, I'd fall into the open maw of a volcano. No one would know. No one would care. Marcia would never know what happened to me. I'd be D. B. Cooper. Suddenly, he grinned and put the gun down. I backed down the ladder, trembling the whole way. It was a crack in my resolve, but it would take a while longer for the dam to break.

Volcán Masaya in Nicaragua.

There were times when I witnessed poverty beyond measure. My lawyer and I were sitting at an outdoor café once when an elderly woman and her daughter, who I estimated was older than me, asked us for change. It looked like these women hadn't eaten or slept in weeks. They were broken, and it broke my heart. I offered them some money, and my lawyer asked me why I would do such a thing. "They need help," I told him. "There are too many to help," he said. I also remember coming across a little girl at a local hospital. She was blind and deaf, and you didn't need an MRI to see the tumors protruding under her skin. She was dying, plain and simple. I looked at her mother and father, left the hospital, and found a local street bazaar. I found this ridiculously fuzzy stuffed animal toy, bought it, and went back to the hospital to present this little gift. Although she was blind and deaf, she felt the toy for a second and then grasped it hard, making all sorts of squealing noises. I cried. The parents cried. The nurses cried. I learned later that she passed away a few weeks after I gave her my little gift. In Nicaragua, the people weren't underprivileged or economically disadvantaged— they were dirt poor and desperate. It's no wonder I was having a hard time convincing doctors, who were independent and not part of a state healthcare system, to buy what I was selling.

There simply was no infrastructure to support what I was trying to do. Then, in a moment of desperation masking itself as inspiration, I had an idea. There was one group of people with a healthcare system in Nicaragua. One group that could make the difference in our business. One group that, if I could convince them, could turn our piddling failure into a break-even success.

The Sandinistas.

"How do you get in touch with the military?" I asked my fixer and lawyer. He thought I was crazy—not just that's-a-crazy-idea crazy but you-are-asking-to-die crazy. But I persisted, and eventually he managed to get an invitation to meet with the head of the Sandinista military health organization, a man named Chamorra.

On the day of the meeting, the lawyer, our doctor partner, and I packed into a car and drove deep into the jungle. They were both nervously quiet, and I remember oscillating between confidence and terror. We arrived at a giant rusty metal gate that blocked the dirt road. I got out, walked to the gate, and banged it loudly. It all happened so fast that I have little recollection of how I ended up pressed against the gate with a gun in my ribs and several more pointed at me and the others I was with. I will never forget the sensation of looking up into the barrel of a gun and hearing the guards screaming at me. I began shouting, "Chamorra! Chamorra!" It was the name of the man I was there to see and the extent of the language I was able to muster in that panicky moment. It felt like an eternity before the guns were pulled away and I was let go, but it was probably no more than a minute or two.

The crack in my resolve widened.

The guards took us through the gate, up a path, and into what can only be described as a dreamscape. There was a small white house and a lush yard ringed by a white picket fence. Servants in white suits and white gloves escorted us to a table set with tea and crumpets, where we met with General Chamorra, the head of the Sandinista military health organization and a medical doctor. We talked for a long time about a deal, and I found him to be smart and sophisticated, even elegant. He was polite and gracious, and although I thought we had an arrangement, absolutely nothing came from it.

At this point, our clinic was seeing three, maybe four, patients a day, and I think I saw the end of the road ahead. But, still, I pushed on. I don't quit ... well, sometimes.

The final straw came on my next, and last, trip. When I was in the clinic and nearing the end of my visit, my bodyguard (yes, I had one of those most of the time) came to warn me that a riot had broken out in the city between the police and the taxi drivers. I needed to leave—now. He handed me a sawed-off shotgun, shoved me into a truck with two non-English-speaking men, and sent me to the airport. We drove through the riot area, burning cars and all, and finally made it to the airport. I got on a plane and remember looking out at the runway and wondering what the hell I was doing there. I flew home, landed in Miami, and called Steve Schulman from a pay phone—I was done.

My son Max had been born a year before. I was tired. I had come too close to death too many times, and it was time for the adventure to be over. It was time for Paradigm Healthcare to fold and for me to figure out what came next. I called my Nicaraguan attorney the next day, sent him money to take care of my staff, and I never went back. I left an MRI machine in a building. Done.

I often wonder if my name is on some criminal list in Nicaragua, and I promised myself on the plane that I'd never go back, just in case. Leaving an MRI in Managua is one of the biggest black marks on my career, and I've often wondered what happened to the machine. By this time, I had three viable projects. The MRI center in Trinidad, a cardiac catheterization lab in Trinidad, and an MRI center in San Pedro Sula, Honduras. I haven't talked any about San Pedro Sula, but it was a moderately successful joint venture between us and some radiologists. We had a few who's-really-in-charge issues, but overall it was a fun project with some nice people.

MRI imaging center in Trinidad and Tobago.

After telling Steve that I was done, I had to find us an exit. I sold the San Pedro Sula site to our partners at pretty much a breakeven, take-over-the-debt scenario price, and I found a buyer for the two Trinidad projects. In total, we netted about $1 million. Steve, to his credit, gave me my third. He put the remainder of the debt, which he could have saddled me with and left me with nothing, on his other company. He had taken a chance on me three years earlier, supported me through the whole thing, and left me with a hook on which to hang my hat.

He even tried to convince me to come back and partner with his new company, Premier. I thought about it, but I couldn't. I had tasted the freedom of entrepreneurship and could no longer go back to punching someone else's clock. I had a little bit of a runway to work from thanks to his generosity and enough consulting contacts to pay the bills. I was far from rich, but I had a wonderful wife, a beautiful son, and a sense of an owner's perspective.

I did work here and there and plotted my next move. I made an investment, back in Texas, that was supposed to bring me monthly dividend checks—mailbox money—that didn't really work out the way it was envisioned. Which is why, a short time after surviving my adventure in international business and militant armies, I found myself moving back to Dallas with a three-year-old son, a three-week-old son, and a somewhat pissed-off but supportive wife. Goodbye, Boca Raton … hello, Plano, Texas.

REDNECK RECAP

The entrepreneur journey can be a wild ride full of fun and adventure. The key is keeping it all in check and knowing what truly matters.

CHAPTER EIGHT

TRUST YOUR GUT AND MOVE

Resilience: Endurance is an essential element of resilience.
Keep on. Persevere. Trust what you know.

Paradigm Healthcare had been an adventure, and although I went into it with big ideas and high hopes, I got out of it knowing that I was lucky to be alive. Literally. But I was also lucky to have spent four years as my own boss and come out with something to my name. I also walked away from Paradigm with a reaffirmed belief that I never wanted to work for someone else again.

The thing I didn't know was what I would do next. Marcia had been supportive throughout my Paradigm years—working, patiently waiting for me as I bounced from country to country more times than could ever be considered reasonable. Both she and her cousin, my investor, partner, and mentor, Steve Schulman, had had my back and held me up when most reasonable people would not have, and I felt a sense of obligation to them beyond those of marriage and family.

My portion of the sale of Paradigm Healthcare gave our family some breathing room but not much. We were far from rich, but I had a little time to consider my next move while consulting and picking up project work here and there in South Florida.

I also knew that the best money is the money that your money makes—mailbox money. I was approached by a friend from Texas, Ted Groesbeck, to look at a potential opportunity he had in the Dallas market. Ted was a deal guy and always seemed to have something in the works. When I met him in 1984, he was the Konica Film rep who called on the hospital I worked for in Lewisville, Texas. He was a great rep, a fun guy to hang out with, and we developed a friendship that endures today. The other person I was in contact with at the time was Grady Hobbs. Grady was an MRI tech when I met him in 1986, and he understood the technology and had great experience on the ground. I'd stayed in touch with both of them over the years and had even helped Ted out here and there on projects. At the time, Ted had a mobile MRI in Dallas, and Grady was managing a group of clinics.

Ted had an upcoming meeting with a hospital that wanted to rent one of the mobile units on a semipermanent basis. That was a little outside his comfort zone, so he wanted me to sit in on the meeting to see what I thought. In case you've made it this far into the story and not realized it yet, I am not a person who is willing to sit on my thoughts. If I see an opportunity or make a decision, I tend not to bow to a sense of propriety and keep my mouth shut. I'm not reckless or a shoot-from-the-hip cowboy, but I'm also not a lead-by-committee type either, and it's probably one of the traits that has helped me get to where I am today.

I didn't like the deal the hospital had put on the table, and I thought they were confused in their decision-making. They wanted to rent an MRI from Ted while they upgraded another machine they had in an adjacent outpatient clinic. I didn't trust that the hospital had the right mindset, experience, and perspective to get the most out of the opportunity. Instead of passing Ted a note across the table or waiting until we were in the car to speak my mind, I changed the opportunity with a single question: "What if we bought the [hospital's] outpatient MRI business and ran it?"

It was a bold concept, but it seemed right. And sure enough, Ted and the hospital board all went for it. Before heading back to Florida, I told Ted that we needed an operations guy and that that guy was Grady. After a bit of coercing, Grady joined us. We used some of the money I had from the sale of Paradigm, Ted threw in a little bit, and we borrowed about $550,000—and Preferred Imaging Inc. was born.

Preferred Imaging's first imaging center.

I went back to Florida with a stake in another company and a deal with my partners that they would draw enough salary to pay the bills, operate the company, and send me a distribution every month. Like I said, money making money is mailbox money—the best kind. I didn't have any interest in getting involved in the day-to-day and had planned to find an opportunity in Florida, where my family and the majority of my contacts were.

But nothing seems to happen as it's supposed to.

For the next nine months or so, I made occasional trips to Dallas, but Grady and Ted really ran the show, and I waited on my first distribution check. While in Florida, I was consulting for a small imaging group and maintaining my contact with Steve Schulman. Eventually, I had an offer from the imaging company, but I really wasn't sure that I wanted to stay in medical imaging in South Florida. I turned them down and quit consulting. Steve also approached me about joining him in his new company. I gave the offer some thought and can remember as clear as glass the conversation we had in a parking garage adjacent to his office. He offered me 20 percent of the new company and a decent starting salary. After thinking for a few seconds, I responded, "I would consider it, but there are a few people in the organization who would need to go before I would join you."

I explained my reasoning, and he said, "Well, they will always do what I tell them to do and you won't." I was tempted, or should I say that I felt a twinge of guilt, obligation, and safety as he spoke. It would have meant a steady income and harmony for my family and what Marcia was hoping I would do, but Paradigm had lit something inside me. Ownership. Setting the tone. Taking the risk and owning the reward. It was intoxicating but not in the way power can be. It was more about the freedom of working for myself than the monetary gain.

I politely turned him down, wished him luck, and returned to my small office, looking for my next thing. I thought I had time. I thought my monthly distributions from Preferred Imaging would start soon and be enough to carry us through, but they never materialized.

About eight to nine months into the deal, I got a frantic phone call from Grady, telling me that something wasn't right. Something was going on at Tri-City Hospital, where our imaging center was located. All I knew was that there were employees crying all over the place and about forty ambulances transporting patients out of the hospital. I jumped on a plane that afternoon, and when I got there, I learned that the hospital leadership had been charged with Medicare fraud and literally overnight had laid off four hundred employees, transported eighty patients to other hospitals, and locked their doors. Doctors, administrators, nurses … there was no sign of any of them. To make things worse, the next day Dallas police handed Preferred Imaging a notice saying that we had ten days to vacate the premises. The center was on hospital property, which had been seized, and the certificate of occupancy was no good. The utilities were shut off a few days later, and we faced losing our MRI machine due to it imploding or exploding in a quench (sudden loss of helium due to no power). It was literally a ticking time bomb of physical and financial ruin.

If we didn't get the power turned back on, the machine would be ruined. Even if we could get the power on, we still had to find a new place for it to go. We needed help, and we needed help right now.

Knowing we now had about eight days left, we reached out to everyone we could think of, but we really needed help from the city government. They were in control of the utilities and the eviction process. I tried furiously to get in touch with someone, anyone, who might be able to help. We were down to our final hours when we decided to throw a Hail Mary. I'd gone back to Florida, but there was a city council meeting scheduled for the ninth night of our ten-day window. I got back on a plane, and while I sat in the back with my heart pounding, I wrote an impassioned speech that I hoped would get the attention we so desperately needed.

Ted signed us up for the public comments portion of the meeting, and we sat for hours while the council conducted its business. It was clear that the politicians of Dallas had a lot on their minds, but helping us was not one of them. We had been ignored at every step as the elected and appointed officials seemed to prefer the political points associated with being tough on everyone and everything associated with the crooked hospital than helping the three of us, who were in the midst of a royal screwing from it.

The public comments section seemed to bring out the crazies. Sure, some people had legitimate questions, but before we got our three minutes, we had to listen to people rant about aliens (I'm talking space creatures), conspiracy theories, and every manner of crazy. Some people, it seems, just need to feel heard. When it was our turn, I stepped to the mic and identified myself. I began speaking but was cut off by the mayor, a real jerk, and was told I was not allowed to continue. Because Ted had been the one who signed the speaker's sheet, he was the one the mayor and city council would hear from, not me.

I'm not a violent man, but in that moment, I was ready to leap across rows of chairs and smack the smug look off the mayor's face. Instead, I simply looked at Ted, handed him my speech, and said, "Read it." Ted read my statement, which ended with an appeal for help, and was greeted with indifferent silence before they called the next person. The Dallas City Council was content to let us burn.

I grew up in church. Every Sunday and several other times a week. But it was 2001 before I met an angel.

Ted and I were walking through the parking lot, spitting mad, licking our wounds, trying to figure out a plan, and slowly coming to the realization that we were screwed. I was so angry that I didn't notice the first few times the man called after us. When he finally caught up to us, I'm not even sure I asked his name. If I did, I can't remember it now, but he said he worked in the city manager's office. He had heard what Ted had said and had seen the way the city council had turned us away. He thought he could help and asked us to call his office in the morning.

Praise the Lord!

This mystery man got the power turned on, which prevented the MRI from quenching—basically self-destructing. He also helped us get our own certificate of occupancy, and boom, we were back. Back to what, I wasn't sure, but at least we could do a scan. An imaging center, next to a dead hospital that had no doctors in any of their office buildings. Time for another crazy move.

Max and Joey Webb, 2003.

I went back to Florida knowing that my dream of mailbox money was gone. I had invested a lot of what we had in Preferred Imaging, which, through no fault of my partners, was now forced to start over. Marcia had been hoping I'd take a job with Steve or at least be able to be home. Max was almost three and our son Joey was on the way. I hadn't expected to be in the position I was in, but I knew that if I didn't get involved in Preferred in a real way, we were going to lose almost everything we had.

I still remember telling her, "Honey, I know you're seven months pregnant and that I promised you I'd never ask you to move to Texas, but ..."

To her credit, she didn't bat an eye and understood. Marcia was keenly aware of the relationship between sacrifice and success. She understood deep down that the life we wanted required a big down payment. She may have hated the idea of Dallas, but she got on board.

Marcia told me we had thirty days to sell the house in order to get to Dallas before Joey was due. It sold in five days, so we went to Dallas in January, bought a house in the suburb of Plano, Texas, and found a doctor for her and the soon-to-be-here baby boy. But shortly after the ink dried on those contracts, Marcia went into preterm labor and was forced to stay on bed rest, in Florida, until after the baby was born. We couldn't move, but we couldn't get out of our contracts either. While I was desperately trying to keep Preferred Imaging from total ruin, I found myself with a very pregnant wife and an almost three-year-old son and having to pay for the mortgage on the place we sold, the mortgage on the place we bought, and the rent on a house we negotiated with the people who bought our place in Florida.

No problem, right?

As I would learn over the next few years, those were easy problems to deal with. While my first experience as an entrepreneur had been an adventure, my new one was a never-ending series of problems, wins, challenges, and solutions that would require sacrifice, determination, trusting my gut, and more than a little resilience to survive.

My son Joey was only three weeks old when we moved to Texas. Preferred Imaging had escaped catastrophe, but we were a long way from being out of the woods. I don't know if I was aware of exactly what needed to be done, but I remember realizing that it wouldn't be easy. We got the boxes unpacked, and Marcia, who was a partner in every sense of the word, got to work building a life for us in Dallas while I got to work trying to get our only hope unscrewed. I remember kissing her on the cheek and telling her and the boys, "It's time to go to work, so I'll see you in four or five years," which is basically what it would end up taking to get us to where we needed to be. She understood the value of delayed gratification. She understood that an extraordinary life was on the other side of personal sacrifice. That didn't make it easy, and we were far from perfect as a couple—we fought and argued like anyone else—but we endured.

Endurance is an essential element of resilience. The ability to take punishments, make sacrifices, and survive are important traits of the resilient, and Marcia had it in spades. But neither she nor I were masochists. We didn't choose the difficulty of life in Dallas out of some sense of martyrdom or for the challenge of the thing. We did it because, if we didn't, we would have been in real trouble. There were no other options. If Preferred Imaging went down in a ball of

> **THE ABILITY TO TAKE PUNISHMENTS, MAKE SACRIFICES, AND SURVIVE ARE IMPORTANT TRAITS OF THE RESILIENT.**

flame, which it almost literally had, there was no bailout. It was on me and my partners in business and life to get things back on track.

101

REDNECK RECAP

Mailbox money can be cool, but it cannot be your focus. No one can do it better than you can, so pick up the pieces and just do it.

CHAPTER NINE

SUCKER PUNCHED
BUT NOT OUT

*Resilience: When you get knocked down, you can withdraw
and declare never again. But triumph comes from
getting up and trying again and again and again.*

Marcia was a trooper. She made friends for us at the synagogue, and she took care of the boys. We'd have Shabbat dinner together on Fridays and did our level best to honor Saturday night date nights. I committed to being a coach when sports entered the picture, and even through the hardest business years, I'm proud to say that I managed to coach seventeen seasons of soccer, basketball, T-ball, and baseball for my sons. But most of the rest of my life was spent in the car—where I ate terribly, leading to fifty extra pounds around my middle—in meetings, on the phone, or staring at a computer screen. Marcia built a community, found a temple that didn't mind her goyish husband, selected schools, and built friendships—she did everything so that

I could focus seven days a week from dawn until midnight on the company, which was in dire straits.

Ted and Grady were willing to let me be the "boss," and I think they realized that their best bet for solvency was to not put up a fight about leadership but to focus on what they did best. The plan of getting checks in the mail once a month was long gone. We were paying ourselves from borrowed money, and I made small withdrawals from what was left from the sale of Paradigm Healthcare to keep the lights on and a roof over our head. Anyone who falls in love with the dream of entrepreneurialism and its upsides needs to also realize the nightmare of uncertainty and fear that go along with it. There were only so many months that the savings account would keep us fed. After that, I'd be back to square one, with even less than I started with and a giant failure on my résumé, my conscience, and my soul. The entrepreneur's trick is to turn things around and win before the clock runs out.

> **THE ENTREPRENEUR'S TRICK IS TO TURN THINGS AROUND AND WIN BEFORE THE CLOCK RUNS OUT.**

The first step was to figure out where our clientele would come from, since there were no more doctors in the Tri-City market. We focused on the two surrounding markets of Mesquite and Oak Cliff. In Mesquite, we targeted the two local hospitals. In Oak Cliff, we opened up a satellite office with just an X-ray and CT scanner. The second piece of the puzzle was a new borrowing source. Although most banks are slow to invest in start-ups or to give loans to unqualified applicants, there were industry-specific companies that we used to borrow funds to upgrade our machine and set up an imaging center in a rough part of South Dallas.

Anyone in a business that involves brick and mortar knows that you can't and shouldn't be content with a single location. If something goes wrong, you have nothing else to fall back on. A fire, a malfunction, a piece of equipment goes down, and the cash flow stops—and business, my friends, is all about cash flow. Once it looked like the first center was going to be OK, we decided to add MRI to the second location in Oak Cliff. To do so, we had to refinance and take out a loan for equipment and all the other necessities. As I said, traditional lenders would not do this, but then we found DVI Financial Services.

DVI was another lender specializing in our industry and was willing to take our progress in the first location as a sign of good things to come. The fact that I was an industry veteran and had borrowed from them before didn't hurt either. They gave us the money we needed, but DVI now owned us. They were involved in everything, including factoring our receivables, which meant that when checks were written to us, they were sent to a lockbox owned by DVI, who would collect them. A couple of days later, cash—about 80 percent of the receivables—would be in our account. It was a pain, but it was what we signed up for, and it gave us the runway to build the business we had wanted to create all along.

Our business was growing because of one bedrock core belief—provide an experience for patients that gets them talking. Hospitals having MRIs was becoming more and more standard, but hospitals focus on the doctors' needs, not the patients'. They move slowly. They grind patients up in the gears of their own machinery. We needed patients to go back and tell their doctors how well they were treated. We needed doctors to tell their friends how quickly we got results back to them, and the better we did at these things, the more our business grew. It was the same lesson I'd learned time and time again in my career going all the way back to those potholders I sold on the church lawn. If mine were prettier, then the people would buy them.

This devotion to customer satisfaction led to an innovation that I'm particularly proud of, although it's not one that gets a lot of credit.

In our second location, I looked around and saw people waiting before and after their scans with nervous looks on their faces. I'd once seen an MRI machine, at a convention, with a few clown stickers on it and remembered a trip to the dentist where the staff had put posters and a TV on the ceiling to keep their patients calm. A lot of our patients were kids, and the idea hit me like a lightning bolt—let's paint the machines so that they looked less intimidating to people. We ended up decorating the whole room, including painting the machine. Our first one in Oak Cliff was an aquarium theme. Pirate scenes. Beach scenes. Walking into one of our labs was like stepping onto a Hollywood set, and the results were clear. Our patients left with smiles on their faces. We didn't simply make the experience less terrible; we made it enjoyable.

Our painted MRI machine in the Oak Cliff clinic in Dallas, Texas.

And it wasn't just the patients who liked us. The doctors did too. We didn't have big competitors. Our competition was mostly hospitals, where a lonely radiologist would read the results for every department. We decided to hire a specialist radiologist to read the results for doctors. This heralded the arrival of RCND, a prominent radiology group I had worked with back in my mobile MRI days. If a neurologist ordered a brain scan, the results were read by a doctor with a specialty in neurology. If it was an orthopedist who needed to know something, an orthopedic physician radiologist read the results. Doctors began to prefer us to even the hospital labs, and the other mom-and-pop shops couldn't keep up.

Our first center in Fair Park (Tri-City) and our second center in Oak Cliff were doing well enough for us to consider a third one in the Dallas suburb of Rowlett. I called Tim, our representative at DVI, and explained the plan to him. We submitted the forms and were initially told no. The credit guy didn't think we had enough going in the other two centers to be able to take on the third. His mind was changed when the president of DVI, who I had known during my time with IMI and Paradigm, heard about my application.

MOLECULAR Imaging · BABY Sophia · DIFFRACTIVE Ultrasound

RT Image

September 16, 2002   Volume 15 Number 37

NATIONAL WEEKLY NEWSMAGAZINE FOR ADMINISTRATORS, EDUCATORS AND RADIOLOGIC SCIENCE PROFESSIONALS

A Garden of Imagery

The art of cultivating a relaxing environment

VISIT US EVERY WEEK AT RT-IMAGE.COM

*Our company made the cover of a radiology trade publication.
One of our first hints at success.*

"That's James Webb," he told his staff. "We're doing the deal."

In business, you're more than a credit score if the right people know you. It was going to take time and money to get the Rowlett location up and running. Our 80 percent deposits weren't going to be enough to get us through. We were going to need more than that to pay our bills and our staff and for the work and equipment we needed to get the third location going. Again, I called DVI and was a little surprised to learn that they were willing to not only let us keep our 80 percent but also withdraw beyond our receipts to get us through—100 percent of our receivables, to be precise. We were racking up debt, but the extra money allowed us to get the third center up and running.

IN BUSINESS, YOU'RE MORE THAN A CREDIT SCORE IF THE RIGHT PEOPLE KNOW YOU.

I had a feeling that something wasn't right, but after a couple of years of scratching and clawing our way out of hell, I wasn't about to let the smell of a little sulfur stop me. The patients were happy. The doctors were happy. The money was coming in … until it wasn't.

About six months after the opening of the Rowlett location, Grady checked the bank account, and there was no money in it. We had not received our deposit from the factoring by DVI.

"What do you mean it's gone?" I was astonished. He meant it was gone, vanished, not there. The checks that we'd dutifully put in the lockbox had not turned into money in our bank account. Payroll was due a couple of days later, and I tried frantically to get in touch with Tim, my DVI contact, but he wasn't returning my calls. I tried calling the corporate office, and I even tried to reach the president who had approved our loan, but it was like they had all vanished into thin air.

Whatever was happening, it wasn't our employees' faults, so Ted, Grady, and I each wrote a check to cover payroll, and I got on a plane to go to DVI's headquarters in Philadelphia. I expected to find that it was a mix-up, a mistake, something wrong with their computers. What I found instead was a small army of FBI agents packing everything that wasn't nailed down into boxes.

109

It turned out that the board members and the CFO of our lender were running what amounted to a Ponzi scheme. They were double-selling the papers on their equipment loans. They would lend money to folks like me and then sell the debt on those loans to multiple interested parties, which, I don't think you need a degree in finance to understand, is highly illegal. To my relief, neither the president nor Tim, our rep, were involved, but that didn't mean they could help. In fact, for all intents and purposes, DVI no longer existed. A company that did $1.3 billion a year in radiology-related transactions was gone in a day. Sound familiar? I couldn't believe it was happening again. Over the next few days, a judge intervened and restored our factoring line to 80 percent, not 100 percent as we had been used to, and the successor to our loan account was now US Bank.

I had ignored my gut before when DVI had allowed us to over-factor our receivables. I'd let my exhaustion, eagerness, and hope that things were turning around silence my inner voice, and on the flight home, I heard it talking to me again. This time I listened.

Something told me that there had to be a separation, a physical barrier put between us and whatever entity would ultimately hold our loans. I don't know where the idea came from, but I called Grady from the car on my way home and told him to go to the post office the next morning and get a post office box. I also told him to change the accounts-receivable address from the lockbox to the PO box. He did, and after about thirty days, checks started showing up in the PO box instead of the bank lockbox. Grady would then leave work every day, pick up our checks from the post office, and deposit them into the bank's lockbox on his way home.

My gut was way ahead of me, and I'm glad I listened. No one knew. From the perspective of the successor bank, US Bank, checks were in the lockbox, and they were financing 80 percent of the amount. But we had that extra step that we kept hidden for a long time.

We thought we could live with this and proceeded to build the company as we had planned. All three centers were up and running, and every night Grady would stop by the PO box to pick up the checks before taking them over to the lockbox. Things were going OK, and my gut and I were in sync. For a few months, anyway.

It turned out that we weren't done walking through hell quite yet.

After taking over our loan, things with US Bank seemed like they were going to work out OK. They didn't know anything about our industry, but I didn't worry about the FBI raiding their offices and freezing their assets. As long as they left us alone, we'd be fine and we'd get back on our feet and pay back the DVI loan to US Bank—or so I thought, until the foreclosure notice and lawsuit showed up. Apparently the lawyers and geniuses at US Bank decided that, since DVI had allowed us to overfactor our receivables, we were in default of our loan. They filed a lawsuit for $3.6 million against Preferred Imaging and also against Ted, Grady, and me, individually.

They say the hand of justice is swift, but let me tell you, the US legal system is anything but. The lawsuit dragged on for almost two years. All the while we kept the centers running, and every night Grady made the post-office-to-lockbox run. We had sunk more than $500,000 into the defense against the lawsuit and were throwing good money after bad. Finally, I'd had enough. I did some math and figured that I could come up with half of what the bank wanted. The lawyer prepared the settlement offer and took it to US Bank, who thought it would be a better idea to press for the whole thing. What did they care? They were getting our receivables anyway, and the longer the thing dragged on, the more profitable the $3.6 million would be for them … or maybe they just loved watching the little guys suffer.

At least, that's how it felt while I was sitting across a table from a pompous US Bank employee. One of those guys who thought he was hot shit just because he wore a suit and tie and could mess with us. The meeting went nowhere, and the US Bank guy really played the asshole card. No settlement—pay it all or lose everything.

By the time I got back to Texas from the meeting, I was pissed and desperate. Screw them. Let them come after me. My house was protected. I'd lose a car, what little savings I had, and have a bankruptcy on my record, but I was tired of fighting corporate drones who didn't have skin in the game. None of these guys had ever built anything, and if ruining me was how they got their jollies, then fine … fuck 'em.

I called Grady and told him not to put the checks in the lockbox. I told him to deposit the money into our bank account directly. If US Bank was going to shut us down, then we would need some walking-around money while we tried to rebuild our lives.

"How long do you want me to do that?" Grady asked. It turned out that it didn't take long. The morning of the third day with no lockbox delivery, I got a call from my lawyer.

"What the hell have you done? I just got a call from US Bank's counsel, and they want to know why there is no money in the lockbox."

I told him what we had done and said, "I think I'm getting what I can before they take it all away from us."

"You can't do that, James."

"Watch me," I said, and I hung up the phone.

Remember how I said I listened to that little voice in the back of my head that was telling me to reroute the checks to the PO box? It turns out this was why it was telling me that. After two years of obstinance, US Bank accepted our settlement offer of $1.8 million in forty-eight hours. All it took to move the river was to turn off the tap.

But my gut wasn't quite done.

Part of the settlement required us to continue to deposit our receivables into that damned lockbox for 120 days. I was like a kid counting down to Christmas for those four months. The sooner it came, the sooner US Bank, DVI, and the whole thing would be behind us. We dropped off the checks on the 120th day and on the 121st day, we started putting them directly into our bank account. Just what we believe the settlement called for.

Well, it turned out that just as DVI had a specialty in providing financing to small companies in medical imagining and US Bank had a specialty in picking up debt from financial scandals, there was another group out there with a specialty in buying settlements from banks. They give the bank some percentage of the settlement amount and keep the difference over the period that it is actually collected from the person making the settlement. This group, who I will not dignify by naming here, said we'd misunderstood our 120-day settlement period and now owed them additional receivables money, plus a little extra for the trouble.

The whole thing went on longer than it should have, but not as long as the US Bank debacle, and, on a couple of occasions, required my lawyer and me to fly back and forth to Philadelphia where the suit was filed, for a grand total of less than $100,000. We were going to be in court three days, October 26–28, 2008. I remember the dates because it was during the World Series, and the Phillies were hosting the Tampa Bay Rays for games three, four, and five. On October 27, everything looked good to be wrapped up the next day. I was pissed because I didn't think we'd done anything wrong, but if writing these scumbags a check was going to make almost four years of fighting end, then so be it.

I was feeling a little jocular, a little relieved, and I wanted to celebrate. I decided to spend some money and take my lawyer to the

World Series. I got tickets behind the third base dugout—some of the best tickets I've ever had to a baseball game in my life—and was excited to unplug and relax. The Phillies were up three games to one in the series, and I thought it would be pretty cool to see a champion being crowned, but then it started to rain, and rain, and rain. It rained so much that the game was canceled and everyone in the stadium was issued tickets for a do-over a couple of nights later. It was a bummer, but I was heading home the next day with the mess behind me, so I wasn't too upset.

I entered the courtroom the next day, and the judge came in with an incredulous look on her face. She'd been meeting with the lawyers from both sides in her chambers, and apparently there was an amendment to the settlement terms.

"Mr. Webb," she said, "the plaintiff is asking for the agreed-upon sum."

"Yes, Your Honor."

"And they've agreed on the payment terms."

"Yes, Your Honor."

She looked at me with an expression that I interpreted as "Even I don't believe this," then said, "But they would also like your World Series tickets. What do you think about that?"

Anger boiled in my veins. Apparently while the lawyers were waiting to meet with the judge, my attorney had mentioned our adventure to the ballpark to the other side, and they thought they'd try to stick it to me one more time.

"Well, Your Honor," I said, "forgive me for saying so, but there's no fucking way in hell they are getting my tickets." My attorney immediately scolded me for cussing but I didn't care. What a shit move from them to try to tack on my raincheck World Series tickets to a financial settlement.

"That's what I thought," she said. After meeting again with the opposing side, she had the tickets removed from the request, and the original settlement was honored. She was great. Those guys on the other side of the courtroom were real bastards.

My attorney and I went straight to the airport from court and had some time to kill. We were drinking in the airport lounge when I heard my gut start talking. I didn't know why, but I knew I had to do what it was telling me. I called over our waiter, a kid of about nineteen, and asked him if he was a baseball fan. He said he was and that he and his dad loved the Phillies. I asked him if he wanted to go to a World Series game, and he didn't seem to believe me. I pulled out the tickets for the makeup game and handed them to him.

"I just have one request," I told him. "After the game, would you mind sending me the ticket stubs?" He looked confused but took my business card and the tickets with all the joy I could have ever asked for.

A couple of weeks later, a letter arrived at my office. It was from the kid. He wrote about the incredible seats and how grateful he and his dad were for them. He told me about the excitement of seeing their team win the World Series from the best seats in the house and thanked me again about a hundred times. Enclosed were the used game tickets, just as I'd requested. That's when I knew why my gut had told me to ask for them. I went over to the desk and pulled out the settlement details and my checkbook. I wrote a check for $95,000 and a note that simply said, "Here's your fucking World Series tickets." I put the check, the tickets, and the note in a FedEx envelope and had a little chuckle to myself. A few days later, my lawyer called me and said opposing counsel had called him. Everyone was laughing, and they said it was the greatest fuck-you they had ever seen. At least I had some satisfaction.

The sacrifice and hard work of the previous years was ready to give way to prosperity. The company had already grown in the time it had taken to settle the lawsuits, but resilience built on endurance had honed my gut just as experience had honed my thinking. And now it was time not only to endure but also to thrive.

REDNECK RECAP

Sometimes things come out of left field and can be devastating if you let them. Don't.

CHAPTER TEN

Prosperity

HARD WORK AND PERSEVERANCE PAY DIVIDENDS

*Resilience: What looks like luck to others is often
the result of hard work and perseverance.*

Preferred Imaging may have gotten off to a rocky start, and the challenges in the last chapter certainly made things difficult at times, but that doesn't mean that the business wasn't working. In fact, once we righted the ship, it was the exact opposite. It seemed like opening a private imaging center in a relatively untapped market was the right idea for the right time.

Neither I nor my partners had to spend a lot of time chasing deals after we got up and running with the first center. The deals came to us. After seeing the kinds of service and results we were providing to patients, doctors came calling. Our third center was in Rowlett, Texas. Our plans must have leaked out, because a local hospital administrator in the area heard about us and our interest in expanding. He invited me to lunch to talk about our plans. I thought I was going to meet with him about a potential partnership, but it turned out that he had something else in mind.

As we drank iced tea and waited on our food, he smiled and said, "I'm glad you agreed to meet me. I wanted to warn you that if you build your center in Rockwall, we'll shut you down." He was smug, the exact kind of guy I hated working with in hospitals. He was self-righteous and superior. He thought there was no way a little company like ours could out-serve, out-price, or outmaneuver a big, shiny hospital like his. He wanted me to know it, too, which is why he requested a face-to-face meeting—the preening peacock, showing off what a big, important man he was and trying to put fear into me.

What he didn't count on was that his toothy little warning had the exact opposite effect. I had been held at gunpoint by the Sandinistas, nearly lost everything when a hospital just like his was busted for fraud, and knew that people don't warn you when they are confident. They warn you when they are scared. Our focus on patient experience and delivering results faster, more accurately, and with greater expertise to the doctors who needed them were a big threat to the hospital's slow, impersonal, and arrogant approach. He may have asked me to lunch to scare me out of expansion, but all he did was confirm that Preferred Imaging was on the right track.

We built the Rockwall location anyway. And then Casa Linda, and Richardson, and Grapevine, and twenty-four other imaging centers across Dallas and around the country. And almost all of them began with calls from doctors looking for something better than what they were getting from hospitals, and all of them were the antidote to that administrator's warning. At almost every step in the process, we took a step away from conventional wisdom. We limited our amount of lower-reimbursing insurance plans, and we focused on the higher-end managed care plans that offered better benefits to their clients and better payments to us. We excelled at marketing and customer service, ensuring that both our referral base and our patients received the utmost in service and treatment. We expanded our offerings to bring more people in the door for these added services.

I recognized at an early stage that we needed diversification and multiple revenue streams. Our first step in that direction was building a pain management treatment facility. At the time, there were only two options for treating chronic pain—take addictive medication or go to a surgery center or hospital for an injection in the spine. For people with chronic pain, neither was a great option. The drugs, in addition to being addictive, can be really hard on the body if taken over a prolonged period of time. Hospitals and surgery centers are expensive—expensive to build, expensive to maintain, expensive to visit as a patient. We developed an alternative. We built a pain procedure center at our Richardson location. Think of it as a surgery center light for outpatient procedures. We had all the accreditation of a surgery center, but we did procedures that did not require a licensed facility, so we provided a high level of care for a lot less money.

All the physicians who used our facilities specialized in pain management and specifically in spinal injections. A patient would arrive, be prepped by the nursing staff, and be given light sedation, known as conscious sedation. The physician performed the spinal injection and then the patient went through recovery, was evaluated by the doctor and staff, and, when ready, was sent home. Our specialty was ensuring the highest care while getting folks in and out at a healthy pace. At our peak, we were servicing fifty-three practices through nine facilities.

Insurance companies eventually started pushing back. Our model was built on innovation, and innovative things seldom fit into the clean-

tracting, and business development. That meant sacrificing the usual trappings of success in favor of a future of abundance. I worked from a desk next to a bathroom in the back of one of our centers. Our "offices" for the first few years were open spaces wherever we could find them. I worked out of my car. I delayed gratification and remuneration based on the belief that the right decisions in the early stages would mean flexibility down the road.

At Preferred Medical Holdings, we fostered a work-hard, play-hard mentality: have lots of fun, but get the job done. This photo is from a 2010 management retreat.

We could have made decent livings with one or two imaging centers. We could have worked nine to five, lived in decent houses, and played some golf. But we, or at least I, knew that prosperity is a function of delayed gratification and growth. You could set up a lemonade stand for five bucks a day, bring in eight, and be happy with three. Or you could set it up for five, bring in eight, and then take the three and roll it into a second location and make six. It would take longer but would yield bigger results. It all depends on your intention.

I'm often asked at what point I realized that I had made it, that I had become successful, and I always answer that it depends on how you define success. For a lot of people, success and satisfaction are about money. If that's the case, then success came a couple of months after we opened the Rockwall imaging center. The money I had left from selling Paradigm Healthcare was just about gone and I was taking a small salary. Too small. I had put $25,000 into starting the company, and we began by building and operating entirely on borrowed money. Expensive borrowed money. Even though I had a salary, things were getting really tight at home, even as they were growing at work.

At the end of 2003, a few years after moving to Dallas, I was trying to figure out how to pay my house note, so I decided to take a look at the books from the Rockwall center. I realized that there was enough in the bank for the three of us to make a distribution and take a $9,000 dividend from the business. I won't say I was stunned, but there was a moment of relief. I wrote the checks, gave Ted and Grady their first distribution, and went home to Marcia. We went out for a steak dinner.

I paid the mortgage and other bills and went back to work the next day. In terms of feeling successful, that was a big day. The next month, I was able to take out $10,000, then $11,000, at one point even approaching close to $1 million a month. Before I knew it, I was able to write a check for more money a month than I could ever have imagined. Is that success? I suppose so, at least for a lot of people.

MONEY IS NEVER AN END IN ITSELF, BUT IT IS A MEANS TO THAT END AND A BENEFIT OF TAKING ON RISK AND SURVIVING THE CRUCIBLE.

Money is never an end in itself, but it is a means to that end and a benefit of taking on risk and surviving the crucible. But I've never been motivated by money. Not when I was a little boy, not when I was working for other people, and not when I was building companies. I wanted it, of course, but I have never made the mistake of confusing gratification with cash.

I am an unabashed, unashamed, and proud capitalist. I believe in the power of the market. I believe that choice and competition lead to the innovations that define modern life. I believe in recognizing opportunities and going hard after them, in the relationship between risk and reward, and that the people who deserve success are the ones most willing, prepared, and focused enough to earn them. I like having a nice home and the financial freedom to do a lot of things other people cannot. However, money is a result, not the goal.

Teddy Roosevelt said, "Far and away the best prize that life has to offer is the chance to work hard at work worth doing." There's a lot of truth in that. Gratification comes from doing the work you want to do and being in control of the decision to do it how, when, where, and with whom you choose. I knew we had "made it" when I was able to get up in the morning and go to the office to run the company I had built. Income and growth may have meant that Ted, Grady, and I could play golf on Fridays—five or six years after we got started—but even then, business was on our minds.

We may have reached a desired goal, but our dreams didn't stop there. More was waiting on the horizon.

REDNECK RECAP

Enjoy that first taste of success ... just not too much. Always keep the end game in sight.

CHAPTER ELEVEN

I DIDN'T SEE IT COMING

Resilience: The things that change your life the most are the ones you never see coming. How you respond makes all the difference between success and failure.

I t's funny how the things that change your life the most are the ones you never see coming. Even in the middle of the uncertainty and stress of building our businesses, I had faith that things would work out. I never doubted it, so when things started coming together, when the money was rolling in and the operation required less of my time—or a more focused use of it—I wasn't surprised. I talk to people who ask me if I was ready for success, if it was hard to adjust to wealth, and I always think, *Hell yes, I was ready for success, and no, it was not at all hard to get used to having money—after all, that's what I'd been working for my whole life.*

No, it's not the things you plan and work for that leave the biggest marks on your life. It's not the things that take time, effort, and energy that alter your life's course. These things are the course. You don't want them to change. You want to move steadily forward and see it through. You grow, you adapt, you learn, you expand, but you don't really change. You evolve.

Real change comes at you fast. Real change is a shark that charges at you from out of the depths, a lightning bolt out of a clear sky, a stomachache that doesn't seem like much but won't go away. Unexpected. Without warning. That's how your life changes. It's certainly how mine did.

It was after Thanksgiving in 2011, and, as we'd done for years, Marcia and I had just spent the holiday with her family and hosted our annual invite-only dinner at the medical imaging conference in Chicago. Over the years, as my businesses had grown, I grew tired of the vendor dinners and getting pitched, so I started hosting my own dinners at the annual conference and inviting those friends and vendors with whom I wanted to hang out, all without agenda. It wasn't a hot ticket per se, but folks did like to join us for a break in what was typically a five-day show. On that Wednesday, we said goodbye to her parents, headed to the airport, checked in, and eventually sat down in our first-class seats bound for Dallas. Hosting a dinner at the show, staying at the Peninsula Hotel, and riding first class will certainly make you feel good about yourself. Yep, top of my game ... again.

I was feeling my normal confident self as we sipped a cocktail and waited to take off. Marcia leaned into me and asked if we could stop by the local urgent care clinic when we landed. She said, "I think I have an upper respiratory infection and may have pulled a muscle doing sit-ups." We landed, drove to the clinic near our house, and checked her in. Marcia had the standard workup, a brief physical exam, a sonogram, and then a CT scan. Given my former life as an X-ray technologist, I asked to view the films from the CT scan and immediately noted three large masses in her liver and a possible smaller one in the mid-abdomen region. I searched my mind for an explanation and decided that they had to be benign tumors known as hemangiomas—troublesome but not life threatening. I reassured Marcia throughout the evening that this would all work out.

Our business involves medicine, so I used every resource I could muster to get a quick but thorough workup. After a few phone calls the next morning, Marcia had an MRI scan and, quickly thereafter, a biopsy. At ten the following morning, I received a phone call. We had our confirmed diagnosis: stage 4 pancreatic cancer. No previous recognizable symptoms, no hints, no pains—nothing—and yet we stood at a crossroad that morning knowing that with this disease, there was very little chance of long-term survival. In thirty-six hours, our world and the worlds of our families and friends were rocked to the core.

As I said, it's not the moments you plan for that change your life. It's the moment when you realize that your wife, who has been by your side, driven you, loved you, and supported you, was now standing in front of you carrying around a death sentence in her belly and there wasn't a damned thing you could do about it. I died a little in that moment. Actually, a lot more than a little. Certainly, the smug self-satisfaction I'd felt leaving the conference was dead and gone, dried up and blown away in an explosion of grief.

When I received the biopsy results and that fatal news, I had to tell Marcia. I held her close as I told her, and we both collapsed in the bed in a typhoon of tears. After an hour or so, I began the process of sharing this unfathomable news with family and friends. Although our loved ones held out hope for every treatment, every option, and every opportunity, for the next six months, I held her and began what I can only describe as grieving her loss while she was still alive. I was wrecked. I was sad. But I had a job to do.

Once the initial shock wore off, Marcia and I put on our brave faces and started looking at treatment options. Our first visit was to a doctor in Dallas who was a complete asshole, so much so that I almost decked him in his office. This so-called healer walked into the exam room and said, "You have stage four cancer. You should probably be getting your affairs in order because there's not much we can do for you." Marcia gasped and broke into tears. I, in turn, called the doctor an insensitive fucking idiot and took my grieving wife home to look for better answers.

Over the next week, we contacted Northwestern, Johns Hopkins, Mayo, Sloan Kettering, and even the Weizmann Institute in Israel. They all pointed us to one man and one place, Dr. James Abbruzzese and the University of Texas MD Anderson Cancer Center. We had the best of the best, so now it was time to start this journey and pray for a miracle.

For the next four months, we made biweekly treks to Houston, where Marcia endured all manner of treatment and therapy (much of it experimental), but all to no avail. Not even once. During this journey, I tried to remain calm on the outside and provide a sense of clarity and certainty for our fourteen- and eleven-year-old sons, for Marcia's family, for everyone who loved her—and a lot of people loved her—but on the inside, I was a wreck and a shell of myself. I even developed my own method of dealing with all this pain: Take Marcia for treatment, drive home, put her to bed, go to my home office, shut the door, kneel on the floor, and cry so hard I'd throw up. Then I'd clean up, stand up, put the resolve back on my face, and go take care of her.

I had lost people before. Grandparents and friends, relatives and acquaintances, but nothing like this. Being with Marcia, losing her a little every day, was different. It wasn't something that had happened to me; it was a fundamental change in the definition of who I was. I had been on an upward projection, a line tracking relatively constant forward momentum in a singular direction. But Marcia? It was like the line ceased to exist—it just vanished.

She was, as she had been from the moment I met her, incredible through the whole ordeal. Even as her body withered and writhed from the disease and the treatments trying to kill it, she remained focused on her family. That year, 2012, would turn out to be the most transformative of my life, but living through it was like torture in the pits of hell, and I didn't think it could ever get any worse. I was wrong.

On May 20, 2012, we met with Dr. Abbruzzese. He dismissed Marcia from his practice and told us to go home and put her affairs in order. There was no hope left. In a private conversation with me, he estimated that she had no more than thirty to sixty days to live. We were crushed, but somehow, through the tears, we began the long drive back to Dallas.

About an hour into our sad drive, I suddenly had a very sharp and knifelike pain in my lower back and immediately self-diagnosed a kidney stone. I couldn't believe it and thought, *Not now. I don't have time for this!* I downed a few of Marcia's pain pills, and we made the four-and-a-half-hour drive back to Frisco. We got home around seven that night, so I tucked her into bed, checked on my boys, and then headed over to the local Baylor hospital emergency room. Some more pain medicine, blood work, and a CT scan later, I received more shocking news. I didn't have a kidney stone—I had a tumor the size of a baseball and a diagnosis of renal cell carcinoma. Yep, I had cancer. I again asked the doctor to see the films, and once I viewed them, and in some sort of zombielike state, I simply walked out of the emergency room, against much protest, and went home to be with my wife.

How I got home that night in a morphine-induced haze, I don't know, but I do remember sitting in my driveway for a long time, trying to make some sense of the day. What was happening to my family? I kept asking, *Why Marcia? Why my family? Why now?* I couldn't come up with an answer that night, and I still don't have one figured out to this day.

The next morning, I went about the business of finding a solution for me while also arranging care, counseling, and hospice for Marcia. A few days later, I met with a surgeon who suggested chemotherapy to reduce the size of the tumor prior to removing it. His hope was that he could save the kidney. I thought about this option for a bit, thought about Marcia dying, thought about me dying, and thought about my children. And then I made the decision to forgo the chemo and simply asked the surgeon to take it all. Kidney, tumor, and anything else that might be diseased. I had no choice. I had to be there for Marcia, my children, and the family. Two and half weeks later, I had my right kidney and a nasty tumor removed. Nineteen hours later, I walked out of the hospital and, again against doctor's orders, was home by Marcia's side. At this point, she could not walk, so my dad built a few ramps around the house, and off we went with her in a wheelchair, walking and walking and walking around our yard, the sidewalk, and our new house. As her condition continued to deteriorate, the family began to come in and provide much-needed support. I remember watching sunrises and sunsets with Marcia while we held hands, and because she could no longer talk, I recounted every story I could think of about our courtship, our marriage, and our life together.

I wasn't sure what my sons knew or didn't know about their mom's condition and her ultimate fate, so I thought it time to have that tough conversation. I called them outside, we sat down next to the pool, and I told them that their mom was not going to make it through this illness but that she wanted them to know just how much she loved them, how proud she was of them, and that she would always be in their hearts. Other than telling Marcia that she had cancer, this conversation was one of the toughest of my life. I still recall my youngest son, Joey, telling me, "But Dad, Mom gave me a thumbs-up yesterday." I smiled inside, because even in her darkest hour, Marcia did not want to disappoint her boys. I don't know how long the three of us held each other and cried, but eventually I took them back in the house, handed them off to relatives, and went to be with Marcia.

Then there were the last few nights. I hesitate to tell this part, for it was truly a scene from a horror movie. One of several incidences will always haunt me. It was about ten at night and the family had gone to bed. It was just Marcia and me, her postsurgical husband, doing the best I could. As I was helping her to the bathroom, she stumbled, and her hand scraped through the exact location of my surgical stitches. I don't know how many stitches were pulled out, but I do know that blood started pouring from the wound. I don't really remember it all clearly, but somehow I got Marcia back to bed and began cleaning up what literally looked like a crime scene. The wound was open, but I had no plans to go back to the hospital to get it fixed. So I fixed it myself. It's amazing what you can do in desperation with some surgical tape and scissors. I was exhausted and I was sad, but at that moment, I knew that I could finish this journey at Marcia's side, and nothing was going to stop me. Nothing!

On June 16, 2012, at 12:37 p.m., with her boys, Max and Joey, holding her hands; her father; her brother; her stepdaughter, Elizabeth; a host of family gathered around her bed; and me, whispering in her ear that I would take care of our boys, Marcia Beth Fischer Webb took her last breath and moved on to a better place where she would have no more pain and no more sadness. We, on the other hand, were left behind to pick up the pieces and to try to make some sense of this tragedy that had so forcibly infected our lives.

The last photo ever taken of Marcia.

I'm sure that, like me, you've seen movies or read books where the rich guy goes through trauma and it forces him to rethink his priorities. Scrooge is the guy you love to hate but finds redemption when he is shown life outside himself. You might be tempted to think that was the case with me, but it wasn't. The truth is that Marcia had already transformed me and was so deeply ingrained in my life—my work, my business, my priorities—that her illness was like a string being pulled and the fabric falling apart. I may have had periods in my life when I lost sight of what was important, but they were temporary blips. I will never apologize for my ambition, but ambition is only as good as the person driven by it. I have been selfish, and I have made mistakes, but I have never been such a fool as to forget what is really important: family, community, and helping others.

> **I WILL NEVER APOLOGIZE FOR MY AMBITION, BUT AMBITION IS ONLY AS GOOD AS THE PERSON DRIVEN BY IT.**

Those were the lessons instilled in me by my parents, and they were the values that Marcia embodied fully.

The next few days were a whirlwind of activities. We held a funeral in Dallas and then a funeral and the burial in Chicago. Per Marcia's wishes, I packed up and sent off our two boys for summer camp. I went back to my parents' house in Mississippi to recuperate from my surgery and to contemplate the events of the past six and a half months.

I was sad. I was beyond exhausted, and I had so many questions in my mind: Why Marcia? Why now, as we were achieving our financial goals? What caused this? Could we have done something different? Did I try hard enough? What reason could there be for God to take this woman away from us? Once again, I didn't get any answers, but I swore that her death would not be in vain and that something good, no matter how small, would come from this tragedy. As I stood next to our small family lake in Shady Grove, Mississippi, I looked to the sky and said, "I promise that your legacy will live on, that I will make you proud, and that you will forever be in our hearts, souls, and minds."

As I walked back to the house, I took a deep breath and smiled for the first time in a long while. It was time for me to get my boys from summer camp, and I could not wait to hug them.

There are rules and then there's right. A lot of times these things overlap, but not this time. My life changed forever when I saw Marcia's first scans. A clock began to tick, and I had spent almost seven months going through the grief of her, for her, and with her. I shudder to imagine what else would have changed had I not been on this journey to the end. I'm glad I was there for her, for my children, and for our family and friends. I wouldn't change that for anything in the world.

And yet life moves on.

REDNECK RECAP

Love, live, and enjoy every day because we do not know what the morrow brings. I sure didn't.

CHAPTER TWELVE

RECOVERY AND RESET

*Resilience: Reset after loss and then find a
way to move forward. Again.*

Marcia left a lot of holes when she passed. She left holes in our hearts, a hole in our family, and a hole in our community. She left a hole in life itself.

It was a harsh reality after she was gone, and I needed to get away, as did the boys. I picked them up from summer camp and we took off. We had no real plan other than to live in the moment and to escape from the current reality so that we could create a new one for ourselves. We went to Canada to fish. We went to the Bahamas to drink rum and sit in the sun. We went to Wisconsin to the Dells, and we went back to Laurel. Of all the advantages and blessings I have experienced as the result of success, the freedom to simply be with my boys and to go wherever the wind took us is the one I appreciate the most. It wasn't just that things were going to change for us but that they already had. Everything had changed.

I felt loss after Marcia's death, but the sadness had dulled over the course of her illness. What started as excitement and intrigue had grown to love and appreciation, growth, and family. We succeeded together, failed together, and grew together, and togetherness became reality. Then she got sick and together changed. She was still there but not. Together was no longer a constant, unnoticed reality but a struggling one. What had been so easy became hard. What had been real became memories cast in difficulty, sadness, desperation, and fear.

Then only memory remained, like an echo bouncing down an empty cave.

The new reality for Max, Joey, and me, for our family and friends, was built on an eroded foundation. Marcia was gone the moment her symptoms took hold. She would never be the woman in the velvet dress and patent leather shoes again, and yet that's all she would ever be, all she had always been and always would be to me.

There were moments on our trip when the boys and I would talk about her. We would laugh and cry and tell stories. There were moments when we didn't have anything to say. As her husband, I was able to handle my grief, but as their father, I found myself wanting to take away their grief, wanting to help them move on, wanting to help them stay present, wanting to just be there.

It was another crossroads in a life marked by decisiveness and choice, adjustment and resilience. When you approach a crossroads, you have a choice to make: left or right, forward or backward. In my life, I have almost always chosen forward, but now for the first time, that choice wasn't clear.

I thought a lot about what to do next. The boys, our family, and our friends were all dealing with the aftershock of Marcia's passing, but I was beyond it. I was already thinking about what was next—for my business, for our family, for my life. It was a way of keeping myself occupied. Idle hands may be the devil's plaything, but an idle mind, particularly mine, is a walking nightmare.

One particular moment stands out in my mind. We were at the Atlantis resort in the Bahamas, and I was sitting outside with my laptop open, doing the kind of thinking you really only do when you're trying not to think about anything at all. It had been a couple of months since the boys and I had left home. I'd checked in with the office, but the team was doing a good job keeping what they needed from me to a minimum and of maximum importance. I let my mind wander over the last year, over the decade before that, and to the years that lay ahead. Would I stay a single dad? Would I do the dating scene, and how would I do it with young kids? What would people think? I had a million thoughts running through my mind.

Someone had told me about it, but I'm not entirely sure that I put the address for Match.com into the web browser consciously. I wasn't looking for a relationship. I wasn't looking for anything at all. If I had a notepad in front of me instead of a computer, I might just as well have been doodling. It wasn't like me to do something absentmindedly, but I did. I filled out the form, set up an account, played on it for a bit to see how it worked, and then closed the site and forgot about it.

We came home a few days later, and I went back to focusing on my sons and our return to life without Marcia. She and the boys had been very active in the synagogue and the community. We talked about what we could do to carry on her legacy. We established a scholarship fund for all the nieces and nephews as well as the children of close friends. We made donations to the synagogue in Marcia's memory: one to provide scholarships for the preschool and one to build a youth lounge in her honor. During this time, I kept the boys involved with the community, not only because it was important for them and a way for them to stay close to their mom but also because it was important to me. I needed that experience, that closeness, as much as they did. Budd, Marcia's father, and I became close and remain the best of friends to this day. Through our relationship, as well as the one I had with Marcia's mom, I saw the true pain of parents losing their child. Like I said, I had nearly seven months longer than everyone else did to mourn her passing, but also I think that losing a child is different from losing a wife. A wife is a partner, a person who existed before you came around, who brought a prior life to your relationship. A child, especially for attentive and loving parents like Budd and Doris, is so much more. You are there from the very first breath, the very first moment, and although a wife holds a piece of your heart, a child is a piece of your everything.

I shudder to imagine the grief that they and the whole family were experiencing and pray to God that I will never know such a burden.

I went back to work a changed man. Our trip hadn't been too long that I felt disconnected, but after such loss, your perspective changes. It had been a year since everything I thought I knew had changed, since we were on that first-class flight on top of the world. Our team had done a good job of keeping things moving in my absence, but everything was now different. My perspective was different. I was different. I knew it was time for a change.

It's funny how resolve works. You make a decision to change one thing in your life and, all of a sudden, you see everything else as changeable too. Nothing felt permanent except for my family. Nothing felt certain except for my determination for and dedication to them. I made the decision to change work, and by doing that, everything else seemed to be up for grabs. I don't know if that is growth or grief, but it is important and profound.

I knew it would take some time, but I wanted to begin moving the company in a different direction, one where it could be sustained in my absence or put on the market for sale. I wasn't sure of all the things I needed to do, but just as I knew that I never wanted to work for anyone else when I began my entrepreneurial journey, so now I knew that, though far from being done, I was ready for a change—with my business, with my family, with my life. Marcia might have been gone, but I was still here. Our boys were still here. As all life does, our lives were moving forward.

We set up a $500,000 endowment fund for a local charity in Marcia's memory to support the work she loved doing for the community—children, education, family—the kinds of things she had immersed herself in to build our life in Dallas while I focused on work. It gave us—the boys, me, and Marcia's family—something to focus on, a way to channel our grief and the feeling of being lost into something positive. I think part of me thought that this would be what life was like for a while—family, community, business—that these things alone would be enough for me. I didn't have expectations beyond that, but it's never the things that you expect that make the biggest dent in your conception of the world. It's the ones you don't see coming.

I didn't see Cathy coming.

It's not like I had been trolling or even looking. I had played on Match.com now and again but never had a date since the day I set up my profile. On one of my lonely days of searching the dating site, I suddenly received a "wink," indicating that someone was interested in me. She was beautiful, a single mom to two girls. She lived in Plano, about seven miles away, and she worked in the safety industry.

I know it seems crass to some people, and there are those who will never understand how I could even consider dating someone only months after Marcia had passed. But I remember experiencing that familiar feeling in my gut, that sudden resolve that had led me from high school to college, to X-ray school, to Dallas, to Florida, to entrepreneurism. Every decision that has significantly shaped my life was made in an instant. No fretting. No pacing back and forth and making lists of pros and cons. Simple, clear, steely resolve.

In a matter of seconds, I decided to wink back at her, but I knew I needed to be careful. It wasn't just me, James, the redneck from Laurel, anymore. There were the boys to consider. They had just lost their mom. And Budd, my best friend and father-in-law, and the rest of Marcia's family. And I wasn't some schmuck. I'm a relatively simple guy, but I'm not so stupid to think that a rich widower with a house down the block from Jerry Jones's world isn't a prime target for manipulation and drama.

I introduced myself in an email as James, a medical imaging tech and single father to two boys, with a daughter from my first marriage. We chatted back and forth, and I quickly figured out that Cathy was a special person—loving, caring, sensitive. She'd been divorced for twenty-two years and was protective of her girls. Emails led to texting, and texting led to talking. Eventually, we had our first date. I met her at a shopping area and did the one thing you're not supposed to do on a first date, or so I have been told. I took her for pizza! I hadn't had a ton of first dates. I married a hometown girl when I was twenty and then divorced and met Marcia. So, not many first dates, but this one was a gem. I've said it a hundred times: "It was my first first date in twenty years and the last first date for the rest of my life." We had a blast—and I needed it.

Eventually, but quickly, it became clear that Cathy was the person she presented herself to be. She was kind and sweet. She understood my concerns and even shared them. I wanted her to know me—all of me, the real me. I wanted her to meet the boys, my daughter, and my family, and I wanted them to meet her ... but not just yet. It was too soon. I tried to keep up my X-ray tech masquerade, but that didn't last past the third date. We'd been out, the boys were not home, and I needed to let our dog out for a bathroom break. I asked Cathy if we could run by the house. When we pull up to the house, my house, a house an X-ray technician probably couldn't afford, Cathy said, "You're not an X-ray tech. I think you're a liar."

I responded, "Yep, you're right, but aren't you glad?"

She smiled and said, "I think I am." I gave her a quick tour of the house, and we went back out on our date.

We dated a few days a week, and after about three months, I wanted to introduce her to my sons and daughter, so I threw a fall brawl party and invited about a hundred guests. Cathy was wonderful with the boys right away, and I was proud that they gave her a chance. I met her grown girls, and they were so much like her—strong and bright and warm. I told Budd and Marcia's family after this party that I was seeing someone and wanted to bring her to Chicago to meet them. I can't imagine that they were happy with this, but they are wonderful people and saw beyond their feelings to consider mine. I can never thank them enough for that generosity of spirit.

It took only a few months for Cathy and me to go from being strangers connected by an algorithm to something more serious, and we continued our relationship for about another eighteen months. I wanted her to move in with us, but I was concerned about the boys. And then everything was resolved on a three-day trip to Boca Raton.

Me and Cathy

I was in southern Florida on a business trip, and Cathy had come along for the ride. At dinner with some friends, we were asked if there was Orangetheory Fitness in Texas yet. I said those now-famous words, "What the fuck is an Orangetheory Fitness gym?" I was intrigued, so I took a class the next day. The workout was cool, but the trainer caught my attention. She bled orange and was so excited about the company. Talking to that trainer and looking around the gym, I saw an opportunity. The branding was amazing. The trainers had this energy I had never seen before, and the people doing the workout ... it was almost like a cult. I told Cathy about it, and she began researching the company.

Once Cathy did her research and liked the idea, my simple proposal was that I would buy her three franchises near us if she'd leave her job, move in with me and my boys, and operate this new business while we took our relationship to the final level.

Shortly after we started this new business endeavor, we purchased the rights to most of the Dallas/Fort Worth market. We brought in a close friend to be our business partner and president of the company. Cathy, in turn, stepped back a bit to focus more on our family and our relationship.

After loss and pain and anger, I had found a new life partner and a new opportunity, both of which would forever change my life—again.

Cathy and I were married three years after our first date. I surprised her with a proposal during what she thought was going to be my birthday dinner. We had a reservation for dinner at a romantic hotel, and when we showed up, our children greeted us and we sat down for cocktails. Little did Cathy know that I had hired the band to play a medley of our favorite songs. I asked her to dance. I dropped to one knee and proposed. Our children surrounded us with love, and then there was another surprise as Cathy's family and friends, many from Houston, came out of hiding to join us. Cathy was thrilled, but the surprises were not over. Next, out walked all my friends who had so graciously been there for me and who had also embraced my relationship with Cathy. All in all, we had about seventy-five people join us for this new direction in our lives, and we had one hell of a celebration.

Just married…

The wedding was one of the happiest days of my life. Family and friends came from all over. There were flowers galore, and we had the top band in Dallas, the Jordan Kahn Orchestra, coupled with a former top-four contestant from *American Idol*. The event was even featured in a national wedding magazine, which, for a poor kid from Mississippi, was like something out of a movie. All five of our children were there—my daughter and sons and Cathy's daughters. My family, Cathy's family, a ton of our closest friends, and even Marcia's family, once again stepping up and supporting me despite the loss in their own lives. I will always love that family as if they were my own. And I will never forget seeing my two boys, Max and Joey, walking Cathy down the aisle and my daughter standing with her daughters as her bridesmaids. At that moment, I knew our wedding was not only a celebration of a marriage but also a celebration of a new chapter in all our lives.

One of the most special moments in my life—
my sons walking Cathy down the aisle.

I have a quote from President Calvin Coolidge on the wall of my office:

Nothing in this world can take the place of persistence. Talent will not; nothing is more common than unsuccessful men with talent. Genius will not; unrewarded genius is almost a proverb. Education will not; the world is full of educated derelicts. Persistence and determination alone are omnipotent.

Coolidge will probably never make the list of the country's greatest leaders. No one is fighting to add his face to Mount Rushmore, but there is a lot of wisdom in those six little words—wisdom born from experience. Coolidge made a name for himself in Boston in 1919 when he became known for his decisive action in the face of a bloody and violent police strike. America was newer back then. The country had risen from revolt and survived the Civil War. The industrial revolution had created wealth unlike any time in our history, and with it had come graft, scandal, and an erosion of public trust in the government. World War I had just ended, and although the US had not been hit nearly as hard as our friends in Europe, we found ourselves wrestling with a new identity as an economic and military power. We were prosperous and naive, growing, and powerful. During his administration, Coolidge oversaw an economic boom while maintaining an almost monastic devotion to his ideals.

He didn't have the finesse of a Kennedy or the steadfastness of Lincoln, but he never lost sight of himself. He believed in the free market and in a person's responsibility to do right, not only in the face of temptation but also in the presence of opportunity. He oversaw the roaring twenties while maintaining a reputation of quiet contemplation.

I have never been accused of being the quiet, sober type, but I have always had a soft spot for Coolidge. Historians rank him in the bottom half of the forty-five men who have occupied the White House, but I have always seen him as someone who wanted to do the right thing, someone who believed in the balance between forward motion and introspection.

After the excitement and celebration of the wedding, and as Cathy and I settled into our new life, I made time to think about Coolidge's quote. Persistence and determination are the fundamental building blocks of resilience, a word that has always resonated with me. Some people have mottos; other people have codes and crests and core beliefs. For me, the word *resilience* has been a touchstone, a source of strength, and the lens through which I view my life. Coolidge was wrong about a lot of things, but he really nailed the idea that, no matter what, you have to move forward. And when the day comes when it's time to take stock, when you reach a moment of confluence and great change and take the time to look back, the best thing you did—the best thing you could ever do—was to persist, to have been determined, to have been resilient.

We don't look back at our lives and see the moments when we failed. We look back and see the moments when we overcame, no matter the odds. It's not our failures or our successes that get us to where we are. Nor is it the lucky breaks, the big wins, or the random moments. We get to the present moment in our lives—any moment in our lives—by getting up in the morning and getting to work. Resilience is always the best course. Persistence is always the way.

RESILIENCE IS ALWAYS THE BEST COURSE. PERSISTENCE IS ALWAYS THE WAY.

Determination is always omnipotent. Maybe not in the moment, maybe not in the immediate aftermath, but always in the end.

I know a lot of people who think they can plan their lives to perfection. They think that if they have the right plan, the right education, and the right job title that they will be able to avoid problems and live in a constant state of achievement and bliss. If they just meet the right person, make the right choices, live in the right house, or drive the right car, everything will be perfect. But perfection teaches you nothing, and if you don't learn anything, what do you have to be proud of?

If I were walking down the beach one day, came across a genie's lamp, and was granted one wish, I'm not really sure how I'd act on changing the past. Do I regret the mistakes I've made? Yes. Do I wish my first marriage had gone differently? Maybe, but without things happening the way they had, I never would have met Marcia. If I had never met Marcia, I never would have become an entrepreneur. Do I wish she hadn't gotten sick or that I had gotten more time with her? Of course I do. But I would not have met Cathy. We would not have this big, wonderful blended family. No way.

My point is that it does no good wishing for a different past or planning an impossible future. Life is not lived in either the past or the future but in the present. The present is what you can control, and it is in the present—in this very moment—where resilience is your greatest asset, where you are defining the person you are, the person you will become, and the person you will look back at with Coolidge's omnipotent perspective. Don't waste your time doing anything but getting back up and pushing yourself forward, because in the end, you won't look back and see singular moments, only motion and momentum.

No one lies on their deathbed wishing they had done less or not gotten back up after they had been knocked down. Don't beat yourself up too much for your mistakes, and don't let your successes make you soft. Instead, get up every day and do the best you can to build on the collective of what you have learned, what you have built, and the time you have left.

Resilience is the way.

REDNECK RECAP

Hold the memories. Let go of the past. There is still life to live, so live your best life while always looking for the next purpose, place, or direction.

CHAPTER THIRTEEN

CONTROVERSY AND THE EXIT

Resilience: Plan ahead, but watch your back. Never let success make you become soft or lose focus. Others might try to take advantage. Be prepared to respond. Keep your eyes forward and your attention focused.

The most satisfying benefit of success was the promise I had kept to myself of never again working for anyone else. The industry around us was changing by the end of the first decade of the twenty-first century. Consolidation was happening. Other people like me were rising to prominence. There was a "James Webb" in Atlanta, in South Florida, in Phoenix, and in California, and more were coming. Private equity groups were buying up players, and we knew that the time to sell our business was approaching.

Ted, my partner, has always been an idea guy. He's a blue-sky thinker, a big-picture guy, not an operator. We were on cruise control and raking in cash, and I suspect that we were a little restless. Some of our discussions during this time centered around why a managed care company didn't own their own imaging centers, and to Ted's credit, he had some contacts with a major player in that arena. I wasn't 100 percent on board with the idea, but Ted was my partner and my friend, so we met with the managed care executives to discuss this idea. Surprisingly, they were on the same page as us and wanted to run the idea up the flagpole.

The feedback was that we were too small for them, but they referred us to a private equity outfit in New York to provide us with growth capital and a potential exit. The PE group was ready to play in our industry and must have liked what they saw because they sent us a letter of intent to buy Preferred Imaging for $140 million. We could take 70 percent of that off the table and roll the rest forward to help grow the company and look for that second bite of the apple. There was a catch, though—we had to go back in-network and contract with all managed care companies. I knew that contracting was mandatory and that it was something we needed to do, but I also knew that we'd take about a 30 percent haircut on our payments and subsequent bottom line. Although we'd make less per payment, our hope was that by contracting, we would see more volume and thus offset the decrease in reimbursement. Maybe I was naive, maybe I got excited by the prospect of a big payout, or maybe I was just tired, but we all agreed, and so over the next month, we contracted with every healthcare insurance company in Texas and Illinois.

I loved the work I was doing, but opportunities like that did not come around every day. Everything was looking good when I decided to fly to Chicago to pick up Budd to go fishing in Canada for a little rest. When I landed in Chicago, there was a message waiting for me—the deal had blown up and the PE group was out.

I never really understood the full story, but I think their withdrawal had to do with several factors. The lead on the PE side left the firm and moved to Puerto Rico to start his own company there, and our reimbursements were down, as predicted. I suspect that the combination of these two factors, and our inability to convince them that we could grow to the anticipated level, caused them to walk.

We had just gone back in-network with our managed care contracts and lost 30 percent of our revenue in the hope of a big payout, and now that payout was not coming. I felt like I had nearly tanked our company on an empty promise. This happens in business. There is no such thing as a sure thing. I got depressed and pissed off at myself for missing the opportunity but also for not trusting the little internal rumble I had about the whole deal. The reality was that it was simply too sweet a deal, and I should have recognized that. A payout of $140 million for the company? It was a big number, but it was not real.

The move back in-network nearly sank our ship, which I took as a sign that we needed a course correction to get back on track. Ted, on the other hand, continued conversations with the private equity group, unbeknownst to me.

For more than a year, Cathy, the kids, and I had planned a big vacation. We were going to Africa on safari. It was a dream trip and one that I could never have imagined as a kid. It was truly a glorious vacation and one that I needed to clear my head and get back to business upon our return. And then it got crazy.

African safari, 2016

We were in the deep jungles of Africa in a camp in Zambia. My other partner, Grady, was in California on vacation with his family, and we had just returned to our camp from a rhino safari when I checked my phone. There was a call from Ted.

"I know you won't agree, but I think that Bob [the managed care executive we have worked with] can run this company better than we can, and he can bring the private equity group back to the table. I'm also having a meeting with all our management team to introduce him to everyone to start the new plan."

Apparently while I was working to get our finances back on track, Ted had been in touch with these particular folks, and they had convinced him that they could operate this company better than I could. Ted was reeling from the PE blowup, just like me, and I think he bought their spiel hook, line, and sinker. His plan was to call the management team together, introduce them to these guys, and get buy-in from the team to revisit the equity group and consider this new management approach. It was a pretty good punch in the gut. He had waited until I was on the other side of the world and Grady was unavailable to try to institute a new plan with new management. Now I was really pissed and had only thirty-six hours to figure out how to stop this bonehead move.

Capitalism can be a rough game. Relationships can be strained, and nothing is ever certain, but I knew one thing for sure—there was no way in hell I was going to allow him to screw up our company with this crazy idea. After the call, I told Cathy, as I had many times, that I had to go. I had thirty-six hours to get from Zambia to Dallas, and I needed every second.

CAPITALISM CAN BE A ROUGH GAME.

I did not even change out of the pants and T-shirt with cutoff sleeves that I was wearing. I took four flights, did not sleep a wink, and managed to arrive in Dallas a half hour before the meeting was to start. During my travels, I had reached out to Grady, Richard (our CFO), and Amy (our head of the company) and discussed Ted's bizarre move. Grady supported me, and as such we had the legal vote to ensure that nothing stupid occurred. Grady has always been a friend and the kind of guy you want with you in a bar fight. Good, solid, loyal, and tough as nails. I had Richard's support also. Richard had joined us in 2004 and had been riding the roller coaster with us for many years. He was smart and honorable and did not tolerate bullshit. Honest to a fault, he bowed out of Ted's meeting and would not be a part of it. Amy literally grew up in the company and went from our first clinic administrator to president of the company. Because airplanes now had internet access, she and I communicated during the entire flight about Ted as well as things happening around the office, particularly that everyone was freaking out and did not understand what Ted was trying to do. PE turmoil and now this. That would probably make any employee uneasy about a company's future.

When I finally landed, I had a driver waiting to take me to the office. I told the driver, an enormous guy named Frank, that I did not care what it took. I had to make it to the office by 2:00 p.m. Frank, who was a gentle giant, must have seen that I was serious, because he hit 100 mph on the freeway trying to get me there. When we arrived, only a couple of minutes after the meeting had started, I asked Frank to join me, saying that he didn't need to do anything other than remain silent and do his best to look like a badass, which, for him, didn't take much.

Thinking back, we must have been quite a sight when we burst through the door. I was still wearing my workout pants and cutoff shirt, which was now covered in blood because all the flying had led to a nosebleed. My eyes were beet red, my hair was a mess, and I was unshaven for more than a week. And standing behind me was a guy who looked like he had been plucked from a line at central casting for a bouncer audition. Ted looked like a deer in the headlights. I had made it around the world in a day and a half to call him on his move. Everyone in the room sat in stunned silence as I politely told the two guys being "promoted"—who weren't bad guys, they had just been led to believe that Ted could control the company—to get the fuck out of my conference room. I then told everyone to go home and that we would regroup in the morning. Ted tried to object, but I told him that Grady and I had the controlling legal vote and that this party was over. Period. I left the conference room and went to my office pissed, exhausted, and hyped up. Ted came in and tried to apologize, but I was too tired and too angry to talk. If we had spoken in that moment, it would not have been pretty and probably would have caused an irreparable situation.

I told Ted to go home and to stay away from me until I had this sorted out. I needed sleep and time to think. The driver took me home, and I called Cathy to let her know what had happened. She and the kids were still in Africa and on another safari. I showered and slept. The next day, I retained a litigation attorney and had every intention of removing Ted from any management responsibilities. After about a week, I learned that I had two options: buy Ted out or fix the relationship.

There was no chance that I was going to buy him out of the company, so fixing the relationship was my only choice. We needed to talk. I asked him to meet me at the office the following Sunday, and when we sat down, he apologized and told me that he had gotten scared after the PE group explosion and that he had screwed up. He was caught up in the rhetoric from the managed care guys, who had gotten in his head, and he apologized again. Then I finally knew what I needed to say.

"Ted, I've known you for over thirty years, so I forgive you. Let's move forward and put this behind us." In my mind, I knew I could forgive, but it would be a long time before I could ever forget.

Ted and I managed to repair our relationship. We had been friends for a long time, and although what he did was completely unacceptable, he was still my friend. I suppose it's a little ironic that I was on a safari when it all went down because, charging into that board room, I felt a little like a lion pouncing to defend his pride. And although I have the heart of a lion, I also have the mind of an elephant. I meant it when I said that I'd never forget.

It was clear from that moment that Preferred Imaging needed to be fixed and that the days were numbered for Ted, Grady, and me. I told Ted that I wasn't going to buy him out but that we would all work together to get the company prepared for sale, which took about a year and a half. I'd learned from the disaster that happened after the PE group signed their letter of intent to buy us out that there's a reason companies hire investment bankers to handle those kinds of deals. Investment bankers and brokers have the skills and resources to do the necessary due diligence and to maintain a distance between the buyer and the seller, which means someone else gets to be the bad guy in the negotiations.

Early in the spring of 2017, I met a Canadian gentleman who was buying up distressed imaging centers on the US East Coast. If Preferred Imaging was the Neiman Marcus of imaging centers, then this guy was Walmart. If we were the Rolls Royce of our industry, he was the Honda Accord. We hit it off and became friends. I liked his vision, and he liked my knowledge of the industry and experience. We needed each other, so I introduced him to our investment banker to start the process of a potential acquisition of our company by this strategic player.

If I have learned anything over my lifetime, it is that you should never get too full of yourself, never get too comfortable with your status or accomplishments. Keep your eyes forward and your attention focused, or you'll never see what's coming next.

By August 2017, the deal was finalized, and Preferred Imaging was sold for $94 million, which was a damned good return on $25,000 and a sixteen-year investment. At that time, it was the high mark of my career as an entrepreneur, but it also fueled my fire to do more.

REDNECK RECAP

Partnerships can fail for many reasons, but we managed to survive and thrive. Sometimes you just have to forgive. It is required. It is necessary. It brings inner peace. It does not mean that you have to forget, and it does not mean that you can't finish your dream with your partners/friends.

CHAPTER FOURTEEN

ENTER WITH THE EXIT IN MIND

Resilience: Everything is about the end. Getting there
takes perseverance, focus, and hard work.
Stick it out until the end.

I f there's anything I've learned in my life as an entrepreneur, this is probably the most important: enter with the exit in mind.

I have met many people who have gone into business with big dreams about building an empire. They design their start-up strategy and have grand plans for the immediate future, but they never think about how it's all going to end.

I've learned that everything is about the end.

The end is when you cash a big check or go home with your tail between your legs. The end is what divides the successful from the parables.

When I began my first business in the Caribbean, I didn't know enough to think about the end. I heard about an opportunity and wanted bought franchises were generally customers who loved the way the brand made them feel, not people who wanted to build a business. A typical franchisee would buy one location, with nebulous dreams of a second or even a third. They started at point A, identified point B, and hoped for point C.

This provided a couple of key opportunities for me. I wanted to build a business, not be an ambassador for the brand. I liked the fitness aspect of Orangetheory, but I personally didn't do the workout. I'd rather hit the weight room and the treadmill with headphones blaring and no one talking to me. What I really liked about the company's passion was demonstrated in the product and in the numbers.

I had access to more capital than most owners, and I knew early on that I didn't want to own one or two gyms but a sizable area, maybe even territory rights to a state. This gave me leverage with the parent company to build my plan.

Going from a couple of locations to securing the rights to most of the North Texas market didn't take long. I can't go into the details for legal reasons, but because I went to corporate with a vision for how I was going to aggressively grow their business, take on risk, and get out, I changed the conversation and the price sheet. I wasn't wasting a lot of time with their basic franchise cost and inclusions. Instead, I negotiated like a person who could afford to walk away.

DON'T LET PASSION GET IN THE WAY OF SUCCESS

This is another big lesson I'd learned over the course of my career: don't let passion get in the way of success.

I don't necessarily believe in chasing your passion as your work. I love fishing and golf, but those are not career paths for me. I believe in being passionate about what you're doing. If I were an "orange-bleeding client" of Orangetheory Fitness, I wouldn't have been able to negotiate the deal that I did. I would have been too wrapped up in it emotionally. If I were excited about the prospect of working on something I love, I would have lost sight of the fact that what I really love is independence and flexibility. The result was that I didn't have to take what was offered; instead, I was able to negotiate my own deal.

Orangetheory Fitness

Once we owned the Orangetheory territory, we then had the right to sell franchises. The idea of managing a bunch of single-site operators just didn't make sense to me. Why would I want to manage multiple franchisees and try to hold them to a corporate standard when I had no real control and no significant economic benefit? I didn't want to be the guy selling franchise rights to dreamers. I wanted to be the guy who built, and owned, an entire region. There's a lot of benefit to thinking that way, but it requires the number one asset in business: access to capital.

When I was young, I would have begged, pleaded, and borrowed to put money together to get something off the ground. Unfortunately, it's a fact that you have to do that to get started. But what blows my mind is seeing people who have been successful continuing to put their worth on the line over and over again, hoping not to get burned.

I'm a big believer in debt. A lot of people disagree with that point of view, but I believe that it's better to borrow other people's money, particularly when the conditions are right, to build your business than to potentially lose your shirt while investing your own money. To do that, you must rely on asset protection—it's my way of life. In 2004, an attorney told me that the greatest thing in life is owning nothing and using everything. LLCs, LPs, family limited partnerships, and trusts are all used by attorneys to create asset-protection vehicles. Once you "own nothing," it is easier to sleep at night when you borrow lender money.

That's not to say that you don't pay your bills. After more than thirty years as an entrepreneur, I have built relationships with people for whom I have created value. Bankers, investors, people who are willing to lend me $1 million over a phone call. Why do they do that? Because I have always paid my bills and have always taken accountability for my mistakes. Even though I am asset protected, I have never bailed on a loan, even if it went bad—but I could and that's why I sleep better at night. It may seem tempting to try to do everything yourself, to limit the number of people involved in your business, but that's a mistake and a road fraught with danger and risk. Capitalism is about relationships, not just about money.

We caught the rise of Orangetheory at the perfect moment, and to take advantage of that, we secured a $10 million line of credit and went to work building studios as fast as we could. We initially built eighteen gyms and then merged with three smaller groups to acquire thirty-one gyms under our control. We still owned the area and had identified at least twenty-plus additional locations. We saw where the business was going and stayed true to our exit strategy. In 2019, we hired Fifth Third Bank to put together a presentation, or in their words, "the book," and put the business up for sale. I knew Fifth Third Bank, and I knew what they were good at, so we worked with people who knew what they were doing, even if it cost us a little money. The investment bank identified 120 potential private equity buyers. Within a few months, we had seventy interested parties, and by the end, seventeen letters of intent.

We worked the vetting process and narrowed it down to three possibilities. From there, we negotiated down to one and started the due diligence and additional negotiation—with the buyer, with Orangetheory corporate, and, several times, with both in the same room. The net result was that, in December 2019, two months before the 2020 pandemic (COVID-19), we sold the company for a very nice payday. With my piece of the pie, I deposited another $20 million in the bank. Another partner and I maintained ownership of the area rights (so that we could sell more franchises to the buyer), and we made several members of our team millionaires.

Seems like a slam-dunk success story, right? Guess what I did the next morning—I went to work. Why? Because I didn't get to where I have helped me to capitalize on those opportunities and to survive bad situations. Strong relationships with banks have gotten me loans when I probably didn't qualify for them. Relationships with mentors and customers have helped me to overcome temporary shortfalls. Relationships with partners and competitors have allowed me to take risks, try new things, and view strategy through a different lens. Relationships with employers and employees have multiplied my output and brought meaning to my work. In life, relationships are the reason for working. Family, friends, communities—without these, life would be hollow and empty.

All relationships require effort. They are accounts that need deposits, not just withdrawals, and gardens that need tending. Be humble enough to understand that you need relationships to succeed, and be successful in developing relationships that keep you humble. Some of the smartest, most naturally talented people I have ever met have achieved a fraction of the success I have seen because they think they can and should do things on their own. That's not the way the world works. It doesn't matter what industry you're in or what kind of family life you aspire to—every business is a people business and every family is a community. You, as a CEO or as a parent, may have more responsibility than other members of your community, but that does not make you more important.

> **IT DOESN'T MATTER WHAT INDUSTRY YOU'RE IN OR WHAT KIND OF FAMILY LIFE YOU ASPIRE TO—EVERY BUSINESS IS A PEOPLE BUSINESS AND EVERY FAMILY IS A COMMUNITY.**

Relationships have always been the most critical thing to me. The good ones have strengthened me and enriched my life. The ones that went bad are like wounds. Healing those wounds stands out as some of my greatest successes.

Backtrack to 1990. Barry O'Brien was my mentor. Long before I began my entrepreneurial journey, he took me under his wing and got me out of hospitals and into business. I adored Barry, and I think he saw in me the kind of person he wanted to help. Working with him was an adventure, learning from him was a gift, and calling him a friend was a treasure.

Until I screwed up.

Our relationship, which had been something I could count on when so much of my life was in question—my first marriage was in trouble, my career was growing, but I didn't have a plan—ended almost overnight. Barry and I had a fight. I was wrong. I had hurt him, abused his trust. I will not go into details, but I went from being his star student to a pariah. After several years of climbing the ladder at Link Scientific Imaging, I was fired six months later when the company was sold. From there came Atlanta, divorce, Florida, and on to my life as an entrepreneur.

I was happy to leave in the rearview mirror so many of the relationships and memories from that time in my life, but Barry stung. His was a wound that would take a long time to heal, and I was too cocky, stupid, or just plain stubborn to do anything but let it fester.

I had been in Boca Raton for a couple of years when I got a phone call from a mutual acquaintance and former coworker at Link Scientific. Barry was going to be in Florida, and he wanted to know if I'd meet him for dinner. I can't remember the name of the place we went to, but I remember that the fancy dinner started off awkwardly, but by the time we got to dessert, we had kissed and made up. I felt a lightness that I hadn't experienced in a long time. We laughed and told stories about the old days. We caught up on family stuff and work and even made plans to get together for golf.

I couldn't undo the past, but it felt like the chance to rewrite the future and include Barry in it had been dropped into my lap. The relationship could never be the same, but it could still be good, and that created a sense of release and happiness in me that I could never have expected. That dinner didn't erase the rift, but it went a long way toward bridging the divide, and it was gratifying to know that the wound had a chance to begin to heal.

It was two or three days later when I got the call. Barry had been skiing with his son not far from their Connecticut home and had dropped dead. I was floored, devastated. Our relationship had been built over years of working together, had come close to a permanent ending in a matter of moments, and, after three years of stagnation, had just begun to show promise ... then this. Just as quickly as he had come back into my life, he was gone, and the sadness was overwhelming.

The funny thing about sadness is that it's temporary. Once the fog started to clear, I realized that the grief had morphed into an overwhelming sense of gratitude. I was grateful to have had Barry in my life, grateful for the opportunity to make up and to be able to look back on the good memories, not the bad. I felt extreme gratitude for my relationship with Barry—not the money we made together, the sales, or the impact on my career. No, I was grateful for him.

That's what I mean when I say that I don't measure success in dollars and cents, possessions, or the kinds of achievements a lot of people seem to think matter the most. When I look back on my life, the biggest successes I can claim take the shape of people such as Barry, Cathy, Marcia, Margaret Love Crosby, Milfred Valentine, Judy Cooper, Steve Schulman, my parents, my in-laws, my children, and my partners. These are the biggest accomplishments in my life. None of them can be reduced to a number, but they are absolutely my net worth.

People are always more valuable than money; memories mean more than money ever could. The greatest accomplishments of my life and career are defined by the relationships with the people who have been a part of it every step of the way.

REDNECK RECAP

A lot of people will be on your journey. Embrace the right ones and thank them often. We all need help.

THE TAKEAWAYS

Resilience: There's nothing reasonable about resilience.
It doesn't make sense to get back up after you've been punched
in the face, knowing that you'll probably get punched again.
But I would rather get back up than settle for the floor.

Business Lessons

Everyone has some silly line that makes the family giggle. Our is "They didn't teach me that at Jones County Junior College." I didn't really recognize what I was saying that until my young son, Joey, pointed it out one time. When talking about overcoming business challenges, new business strategies, or wins, I'd usually end the conversation with "Yep, they didn't teach me that at Jones County Junior College." The fact is, most of my business acumen did not come from what I learned in school. It came from hard work, failure, success, and experience. Here are a few things that they did not "teach me at Jones County Junior College."

PEOPLE

Listen to people. Invest in people. Take the time to recognize people and to hold yourself accountable to people. Whether it is your spouse or your customer, be willing to give to that relationship more than you are eager to receive. Investing in relationships has brought more wealth to my life than the stock market ever could, and I'm glad I didn't wait to "get rich" before I learned that lesson. Start now. If you focus as much or more on your lines of communication as you do on your bottom-line, success will follow. When you meet someone, think about what you can do *for* them and learn from them instead of what you can get *from* them. It's natural to meet and get to know people and recognize opportunities, to think about what they can do for you, but understand that you'll get so much more from the relationship if you think of them as an investment rather than as a target.

If you take nothing else away from this book, let it be this: You and your career will be formed, shaped, built, and defined by your approach to relationships. Everything else is just technique and craft. Relationships are the single most important thing in your life.

WORK HARDER THAN ANYONE ELSE

I don't believe in luck, but I have learned that the harder I work, the luckier I get. Working hard doesn't mean spending more time at the office. This isn't about the appearance of working hard. This is about setting the example for everyone else. When you're exhausted and have had enough for the day, send two more emails, make two more phone calls—do two more things. When you wake up and don't feel like going to work, go anyway. Push yourself, because when your name is on the sign, no one else is going to do it for you, and it becomes really easy to lose your way.

The only thing you can always control in business is your hustle, and the people who hustle the most tend to be the ones who reap the greatest rewards. Don't fall for the modern trap of work-life balance. For an entrepreneur, it doesn't exist. We have one speed—all in—for everything we do. We measure our output in accomplishments, not account balances. Those who want to put in just enough time and work to reach a certain income will lose that income to someone who wants to work harder. It will be difficult sometimes. It will be exhausting. It will mean delayed gratification and personal sacrifice, but the work is the thing that will set you apart, and the benefits will be obvious—both in things you planned toward and in unexpected ones. That's what I mean when I tell people that the harder I work, the luckier I get.

Work manifests opportunity, and opportunities are captured through work. Work harder than you think you can and that effort will take you places you never imagined.

RECOGNIZE THE UPSIDE OF CALCULATED RISK

Just because something seems brilliant doesn't mean that it's worth it, and just because something seems hard doesn't mean that it's not worth the effort. It's easy for me to write this now, in my nice house, at my favorite desk, and with sixty years of hindsight. And, as a concept, it seems easy enough—before you do something, calculate what you will have to put into it against what could potentially come of it. Simple, right?

In principle, yes; in practice, no. I have a pretty good eye for upside and potential downfalls, but it took me a long time to learn how to size up an opportunity and to judge whether the juice would be worth the squeeze.

Part of that is establishing your filters—is a 4x multiplier enough for you to take a risk? Or do you need 10x? Are you willing to invest nights and weekends for the next two years and not have it work out?

Or do you need a sure bet in six months? Everyone has their own preferences and set of tolerances and expectations. That takes time to discern.

It is a bit more immediate to develop the ability to remove biases from your decision-making. Are you so crazy about an idea that it is blinding you to the objective likelihood of failure? Are you throwing good money after bad because of your own sunk-cost bias? Are you ignoring advice from objective sources and expert friends because of dumb pride? This kind of constant humble self-examination is critical to success. You have to be willing to let go of good ideas if they are not worth the time, effort, and outlay, and you must be able to recognize the upside of calculated risk. More than anything, that is the essence of business. I could write pages and pages about how to spot risk and calculate reward, but it means nothing if you haven't gotten your hands dirty and tried it out.

Success is a lousy teacher. Wisdom comes from failure. But wisdom is not the accumulation of knowledge—rather, it is the ability to make these calculations objectively and to stick to your own expectations.

HOPE FOR THE UPSIDE, BUT PLAN FOR THE DOWNSIDE

Today—right now—if everything went to hell, would you be able to survive? Believe it or not, I'm an optimist. I believe in opportunity and innovation, in a future brighter and more prosperous than the present. But I don't let that belief, which is core to who I am as a person, blind me or leave me exposed.

In business, it's easy to let what could be trick you into ignoring the very real possibility of failure. Every entrepreneur does it. They sit down with a piece of paper or a spreadsheet and start to add things up. They see prosperity, accumulation of wealth, a future much brighter than today. That's good. Hope and optimism are the driving forces in entrepreneurialism. But caution is what leads to long-term success. Every business requires a plan, and every great business has more than one plan. There's the plan that lays out what happens when everything goes right, and there's the plan for survival when everything goes wrong. Use the first one to guide your investment and marketing. Use the second to protect your business.

As I write this, the world has been in lockdown for a year. The coronavirus has created unprecedented challenges for businesses in nearly every sector and in nearly every country in the world. Apart from some very forward-looking virologists and science fiction writers, no one saw this coming, and a lot of companies have been put out of business for their lack of forethought. No one will come out unscathed, but the businesses that planned for the upside will be exposed.

Business founders and owners are optimists. Business leaders are pragmatists. Entrepreneurs and operators are both.

REMEMBER THAT SOLID INFRASTRUCTURE IS VITAL

Inexperienced business owners try to do it all themselves. They wear a lot of hats, play a lot of parts, and hope to grow their business big enough so that someday they can do less. It's a natural approach, particularly when you're just starting out—capital is scarce, and you're trying to learn. But experience taught me that infrastructure is everything—it is the difference between someday and success.

Infrastructure isn't about offices or technology. It's about finding the people with the expertise necessary to build the business, giving them clear roles and responsibilities and setting expectations rooted in your plan. In the beginning, hiring people can feel daunting, but financially and in terms of commitment, it is essential. You need help. You need a team. You require support so that you can focus on strategy, planning, and making decisions. You must be humble enough to admit that you can't do everything and realistic and serious enough to admit that you shouldn't.

Putting proper infrastructure in place is a sign of understanding the bigger picture. Details are crucial to success in business, but they can also be something to hide behind. Your job as an owner and operator is not to be every piece on the chessboard but to understand how they fit together and move them to win the game. As an investor and mentor, I will always put my faith in companies with lesser ideas that have the right infrastructure over those based on brilliant ideas without the right support in place. And if a founder with a brilliant idea isn't willing to shift attention to infrastructure, I walk away.

When you plan your business, don't focus only on your offering, your customers, and your finances. Put just as much thought and planning into the team you will need in place for long-term success, and establish that team as soon as you possibly can.

BE CLEAR, BE AVAILABLE, SET EXPECTATIONS, AND CHECK IN OFTEN

If an employee is fired and they didn't see it coming, this is the manager's fault. Barring theft or gross incompetence, firing someone means that you didn't put them in a position to succeed. If a business is struggling, it is the fault of leadership. If someone in a company doesn't understand their role, their job, or their future within an organization, then the blame belongs on the people responsible for putting them there.

I have been asked many times about my secret formula for management, but there is no secret. It's a simple doctrine: be clear, be available, set expectations, and check in often. You can't manage more than a handful of people effectively. Management and leadership require attention and investment, not edicts or intimidation. Set expectations and make sure that they are understood. Communicate changes, concerns, and compliments with equal ease and confidence. Seek feedback. Management and leadership are as much about creating effective, healthy relationships as they are about org charts, and orders have no place in a manager's playbook.

WHENEVER POSSIBLE, USE OPM

I've met many entrepreneurs who fall for the starry-eyed and overly romantic belief that they have to invest everything they have to get a business off the ground. A lot of them end up broke. It can be hard, particularly when you are just starting out, to get other people to invest in your ideas. Whether it's a bank or an investor, you are asking them to make a calculated bet on you and your future. Without a track record of success, that bet looks pretty bad. I get it. Try it anyway. Before you take out a second mortgage or drain your investment account, try to get other people to pay for your business. It can be uncomfortable and difficult to do, but it is worth it. Using other people's money (OPM) may also require you to delay making anything yourself, but it is worth it in the long run. When you use your money to run your business, your decisions are clouded with emotion. You don't make the best decisions for the business; you make them based on a compromise between the company's needs and your own. And if you're overly leveraged into the business, you leave yourself exposed to real problems if things go south.

Protect your assets and keep a clear line between the decisions you make for your business and the decisions you make for your life. Other people's money is a great way to do that. Even when you start making money and put together some capital, don't use it to fund your business. Invest in someone else's business, and let other people invest in yours.

well rounded when you have associate's degrees in a variety of specific areas, a bachelor's in something practical, and the innate thirst for more.

LIVE IN THE MOMENT

If today and only for today you go home and kiss your significant other a little longer, hug your kids a little harder, tell your friends you love them, and go out of your way a little more to help someone, it is a day well lived. I have spent a lot of my life thinking about the future—the next week, the next quarter, and the next decade. It's part of my work and part of who I am. But when I look back on my life, it is never the times I spent wondering about the future that come to mind. It is the times when I was fully engaged in what I was doing, when I was drinking in the details of what was happening at a specific moment in time, that leave the most indelible marks.

You are guaranteed nothing but the exact moment you are in, and you must take the time to appreciate the moment. I realize that it sounds cliché to tell you, probably an ambitious person, to seize the day, but sometimes things become cliché for a reason—because they are true. I don't regret a single meeting I rescheduled to be with my kids. I wouldn't trade a single dinner with friends, date with my wife, game I coached, or moment of being close to the people I love for anything, not money, not fame, not success—nothing.

You lose that perspective when you seek work-life balance. You start to look at the two halves of your life as sides of a scale that must level out. The truth is, when you try to do that, you end up sacrificing both. Work hard, love hard. Plan for the moment so that you can embrace the day. Take the time to think about the gift of living while you work on building your life. That's what makes it all worth it in the end.

ASK WHY NOT INSTEAD OF WHY

I began this book with a question: "Why can't the Webbs be the next Rockefellers?" I knew when I wrote it that the question was ridiculous. It's not a reasonable thought, especially for a poor kid from Mississippi. But reasonable has never been a trait to which I have aspired. Nothing about my life has been reasonable.

Don't make the mistake of thinking that pragmatic and reasonable are the same thing. I'm a pragmatic person. I understand my own limitations. I understand challenges when they arise. I don't try to hide from them. But that doesn't mean that I am pessimistic. Pragmatism is the ability to recognize reality as it is, but recognition does not need to lead to settling. I understand my limitations so that I can find people and strategies to overcome them. I embrace where I come from so that I can appreciate where I am and strive for something beyond.

If you take something from this book other than the perspective of just how crucial relationships are to business and life, I hope it is this: don't be reasonable.

I'm not prone to quoting movies, particularly ones that I don't remember seeing, but a friend of mine shared a line from Cameron Crowe's film *Elizabethtown* that has stuck with me: "No true fiasco ever came from a desire to be merely adequate."

I have faced fiascos. I have had experiences that would scare most people away for good. Getting fired, tanking a marriage, being held at gunpoint, failing in businesses, finding love and losing her to cancer, finding love again and facing betrayal, failure, loss, and misery. In all cases, the thing that got me through those moments was the thing that probably got me into them in the first place—I never wanted to settle. I never wanted to be reasonable. I never wanted to be adequate. If I had wanted those things, then I'd probably still be back in Laurel working in a factory.

If I had let the fear of getting my heart broken stop me, I never would have married Marcia, and we never would have had Max and Joey. If I had let the pain of her death define me, I never would have found Cathy.

If I had sought stability and a reasonable reality, I'd still be working for someone else. If I had let the end of my first business define me, I never would have started another one, then another, and many others after that.

If I had found comfort in my first big payday, I never would have invested again. If I had never invested again, I would not have been able to take care of the people I love when they needed it the most.

If I had let my ego get the best of me, I never would have gone to dinner with Barry O'Brien, and I would have lost the opportunity to heal that relationship before he died.

Be pragmatic enough to recognize reality but unreasonable enough to think you can change it. In other words, in all things, ask yourself *Why not?* instead of *Why?*

There's nothing reasonable about resilience. You would think that it doesn't make sense to get back up after you've been knocked down. But I would rather dodge a punch or strike back than settle for the floor.

Can the Webbs become the next multigenerational business dynasty in America? Can our family survive the pitfalls of generational wealth? Can we change the destiny not only of our family but also of many families? Can we continue to build and grow, plan and give, and contribute and create?

A reasonable person would say no, but I am just the redneck who is unreasonable and resilient enough to try. Resilience doesn't just get back up. Resilience finds a way.